Guiding Those Left Behind
In California

LEGAL AND PRACTICAL THINGS
YOU NEED TO DO
TO SETTLE AN ESTATE IN CALIFORNIA

and

HOW TO ARRANGE YOUR OWN AFFAIRS
TO AVOID UNNECESSARY COSTS
TO YOUR FAMILY

By AMELIA E. POHL, ESQ.

and California Attorney
MARY S. FALK

 EAGLE PUBLISHING COMPANY OF BOCA

The purpose of this book is to provide the reader with an informative overview of the subject; but laws change frequently and are subject to different interpretations as courts rule on the meaning or effect of a law. This book is sold with the understanding that neither the authors, nor the editors, nor the publisher, nor the distributors of this book are engaging in, or rendering, legal, accounting, financial planning, or any other professional service. Pursuant to Internal Revenue Service guidance, be advised that any federal tax advice in this publication was not intended or written to be used, and it cannot be used, by any person or entity for the purpose of avoiding penalties imposed under the Internal Revenue Code (IRS Circular 230 Disclaimer). If you need legal, accounting, financial planning or any other expert advice, you should seek the services of a licensed professional.

This book is intended for use by the consumer for his or her own benefit. If you use this book to counsel someone about the law or tax matters, that may be considered to be an unlicensed and illegal practice. Web sites, telephone numbers and addresses appear throughout the book for the convenience of the reader; however, this information is subject to change as agencies move. Publication of a Web site is not an endorsement of that site by the authors, editors or publishers of this book.

EAGLE PUBLISHING COMPANY OF BOCA
4199 N. Dixie Highway, #2
Boca Raton, FL   33431   E-mail: info@eaglepublishing.com
Printed in the United States of America   ISBN 1-932464107
Library of Congress Catalog Card Number 2005923651

Guiding Those Left Behind In California

CONTENTS

The Organization of the Book

Guiding Those Left Behind refers to the things that need to be done in order to settle an Estate in California. The purpose of this book is to guide the reader through that process. It explains:

1. How to tend to the funeral and burial
2. What agencies need to be notified
3. How to locate the decedent's property
4. What bills need (and do not need) to be paid
5. How to determine who is entitled to inherit the decedent's property
6. How to transfer the decedent's property to the proper beneficiary

We devoted a chapter to each of these six steps; and for those who are in charge of settling an Estate, we placed a CHECK LIST at the end of Chapter 6 summarizing things that need to be done. Once you read Chapters 1 through 6 you will be able to identify those problems that can happen when someone dies. Using those Chapters as a base, you can set up your own Estate Plan so that your family is not burdened by similar problems. The rest of the book (Chapters 7, 8 and 9) suggests different methods you can use to accomplish this goal.

GLOSSARY

This book is designed for the average reader. Legal terminology has been kept to a minimum. There is a glossary at the end of the book in the event you come across a legal term that is not familiar to you.

FICTITIOUS NAMES AND EVENTS

The examples in this book are based loosely on actual events; however, all names are fictitious; and the events, as portrayed, are fictitious.

About The Book

We tried to make this book as comprehensive as possible so there are specialized sections of the book that do not apply to the general population and may not be of interest to you. The following GUIDE POSTS appear throughout the book. You can read the section if the situation applies to you or skip the section if it doesn't. Skipping the section will not affect the continuity of the book.

GUIDE POSTS

The SPOUSE POST means that the information provided is specifically for the Spouse and/or Registered Domestic Partner of the decedent. If the decedent was single, you can skip this section.

The CALL-A-LAWYER POST alerts you to a situation that may require the assistance of an attorney. See the end of this chapter for information about how to find a lawyer.

The CAUTION POST alerts you to a potential problem. It is followed by a suggestion about how to avoid the problem.

The SPECIAL SITUATION POST means that the information given in that paragraph applies to a particular event or situation; for example when the decedent dies a violent death. If the situation does not apply, you can skip the section.

Reading the Law

Where applicable, we identified the state statute or federal statute that is the basis of the discussion. We did this as a reference, and also to encourage the general public to read the law as it is written. Prior to the Internet the only way you could look up the law was to physically take yourself to the local courthouse law library or the law section of a public library. Today, all of the state and federal statutes are literally at your finger tips. They are just a mouse click away on the Internet. To look up the law all you need is the address of the Web site and the identifying number of the statute.

FEDERAL STATUTES
http://www4.law.cornell.edu/uscode
CALIFORNIA STATUTES
http://www.leginfo.ca.gov

California has organized their statutes into 29 different codes, including:
BUSINESS & PROFESSIONAL CODE (Bus. & Prof.),
CIVIL CODE (Civil)   CODE OF CIVIL PROCEDURE (Civ. Proc.)
CORPORATION CODE (Corp.)   FAMILY CODE (Family)
GOVERNMENT CODE (Gov't)
HEALTH AND SAFETY CODE (Health & Safety)
INSURANCE CODE (Insur.)   (PENAL CODE (Penal)
PROBATE CODE (Probate)   REVENUE & TAXATION (Rev & Tax)
VEHICLE CODE (Vehicle) WELFARE & INSTITUTIONS (Welf. & Inst.)

Each Code is divided into numbered sections. When referring to a statute we give the name of the Code and the section of the code. For example, to look up (Family 297.5) go to Family Code section of the California statute Web site and look up section 297.5. If you come across a topic that you think is important, you may find it both interesting and profitable to read the law as it is actually written.

Mary S. Falk, Esq.

MARY S. FALK received her Juris Doctor degree in 1988 from Santa Clara University Law School. She practiced law with a firm in San Jose for eight years, then decided to form her own firm in 1996. She joined forces with Daniel Cornell, an attorney she worked with over the years. They formed the law firm of Falk, Cornell & Associates, LLP, concentrating exclusively on Estate Planning.

The firm regularly provides free educational seminars to the community on the subject of Estate Planning.

As a principal of the firm, Mary S. Falk devotes herself to practicing law with integrity, providing her clients with the type of quality legal service that she herself would seek from an attorney.

Ms. Falk is married to Harry Falk, a Certified Public Accountant. They have three children. Their daughter Serra E. Falk has joined the law firm of Falk, Cornell & Assoc. LLP as an Estate Planning attorney. Their sons Harry and Taylor live in the San Francisco area. Their first grandchild, Harry Falk, V, was born in 2004. Mary and her family are devoted fans of the San Francisco 49ers football team.

Mary S. Falk is a member of the Palo Alto Bar Association., the San Mateo County Bar Association, and a member of the Estate Planning, Probate and Trust Section of the Santa Clara County Bar Assoc.

MARY S. FALK is a member of the AMERICAN ACADEMY OF ESTATE PLANNING ATTORNEYS, and serves as past member of their Board of Governors.

About the Academy

The American Academy of Estate Planning Attorneys is a member organization serving the needs of legal professionals concentrating on Estate Planning. Through the Academy's comprehensive training and educational programs on state-of-the-art Estate Planning law and techniques, it fosters excellence in Estate Planning among its members and helps them deliver the highest possible service to their clients. The Academy provides its members with excellent legal education and top notch practice management support. In addition, each member is required to attain thirty-six units of continuing legal education in tax and Estate Planning annually.

The American Academy of Estate Planning Attorneys serves law firms in over 150 geographic areas in forty-four states. Clients who choose an attorney who is a member of the Academy can feel confident that they have an attorney who is dedicated to bringing them the highest quality of service.

The Academy is also committed to educating consumers on vital Estate Planning issues that touch their lives. Through its series of publications, educational programs and its consumer Web site, the Academy seeks to create a public armed with the information they need to become wise consumers of Estate Planning services.

 THE AMERICAN ACADEMY OF
ESTATE PLANNING ATTORNEYS
http://www.aaepa.com

Amelia E. Pohl, Esq.

Before becoming an attorney in 1985, AMELIA E. POHL taught mathematics on both the high school and college level. During her tenure as Associate Professor of Mathematics at Prince George's Community College in Maryland, she wrote several books including:

Probability: A Set Theory Approach
Principles of Counting
Common Stock Sense

Ms. Pohl, graduated from Nova Law School in Ft. Lauderdale, Florida and established an Elder Law practice in Boca Raton. During her practice, she observed that many people wanted to reduce the high cost of legal fees by performing or assisting with their own legal transactions. Attorney Pohl found that, with a bit of guidance, people are able to perform many legal transactions for themselves. Attorney Pohl utilizes her background as teacher, author and attorney to provide that "bit of guidance" to the general public in the form of self-help legal books she has written. Amelia E. Pohl is currently completing this series for the remaining states:

Guiding Those Left Behind In Idaho
Guiding Those Left Behind In Utah
Guiding Those Left Behind In Nevada, etc.

ACKNOWLEDGMENT

When someone dies, the family attorney is often among the first to be called. Family members have questions about whether probate is necessary, who to notify, how to get possession of the assets, etc. Over the years, as we practiced in the field of Elder Law, we noticed that the questions raised were much the same family to family. We both agreed that a book answering such questions would be of service to the general public.

We also observed, that those who had experience in settling the Estate of a loved one were more understanding of the process, and better able to make decisions about how to arrange their own finances to avoid problems that could arise in settling an Estate. We named the book *Guiding Those Left Behind*. The "Guiding" refers to the guidance that this book gives in the event you need to settle the Estate of a loved one. It also refers to the guidance that you can give to your family by setting up your own Estate Plan so your family is not burdened by unnecessary costs and delays in settling your Estate. We thank all of our clients, whom we have had the honor and pleasure to serve, for providing us with the impetus to produce this book.

THE DESIGN ARTIST

LUBOSH CECH designed the cover of this book. He is a renowned artist, with extensive educational background and professional work experience. Lubosh Cech is the founder of OKO DESIGN STUDIO located in Portland, Oregon. He designs promotional materials for print and digital media. He has received numerous awards for both graphic design and painting. For more information about Mr. Cech and the OKO Design Studio visit his Web site.

http://www.okodesignstudio.com

The photograph that appears on the cover was taken by photographer GENE OSON.

When You Need A Lawyer

The purpose of the book is to give the reader a basic understanding of what needs to be done when someone dies in California, and to provide information about how a person can arrange his own affairs to avoid problems for his own family. It is not intended as a substitute for legal counsel or any other kind of professional advice. If you have any legal question, you should seek the counsel of an attorney. When looking for an attorney, consider three things: EXPERIENCE, COST and PERSONALITY.

EXPERIENCE

THE STATE BAR OF CALIFORNIA has *Legal Specialization* programs in Appellate Law, Bankruptcy Law, Criminal Law, Estate Planning, Trust and Probate Law, Immigrant and Nationality Law, Taxation Law, and Workers' Compensation Law.

To be a *certified specialist* in any of the above areas of law, the attorney must pass a written examination, demonstrate a high level of experience in the field, be favorably evaluated by other attorneys and judges familiar with his work. Once certified, the attorney must fulfill ongoing educational requirements to remain current with the law. To find an attorney who is specialized in the area of law that you seek, call the State Bar of California toll free at (866) 442-2529. Out of state call (415) 538-2250.

Legal Specialization is just one of the criteria to consider. Many fine attorneys are experienced in an area of law, but have not taken the time, effort and expense to become certified as a specialist in that area of law by the California Bar. If the attorney is not certified in that branch of law, ask how long he has practiced that type of law and what percentage of his practice is devoted to that branch of law.

One of the most reliable ways to find an attorney is through personal referral. Ask your friends, family or business acquaintances if they used an attorney for the field of law that you seek and whether they were pleased with the results. It is important to employ an attorney who is experienced in the area of law you seek. Your friend may have a wonderful Estate Planning attorney, but if you suffered an injury to your body, then you need an attorney who is experienced in Personal Injury.

COST

In addition to the attorney's experience, it is important to check what it will cost in attorney's fees. When you call for an appointment ask what the attorney will charge for the initial consultation and the approximate cost for the service you seek. Ask whether there will be additional costs such as filing fees, accounting fees, expert witness fees, etc.

If the least expensive attorney is out of your price range, you can call the California State Bar Office of Legal Services at (415) 538-2267 for the telephone number of the Legal Service office nearest you.

The American Bar Association has a listing of State Legal Service Organizations at the Pro Bono section of its Web site.

 THE AMERICAN BAR ASSOCIATION
http://www.abanet.org

PERSONALITY

Of equal importance to the attorney's experience and legal fees, is your relationship with the attorney. How easy was it to reach the attorney? Did you go through layers of receptionists and legal assistants before being allowed to speak to the attorney? Did the attorney promptly return your call? If you had difficulty reaching the attorney, then you can expect similar problems should you employ that attorney.

Did the attorney treat you with respect? Did the attorney treat you paternally with a "father knows best" attitude or did he treat you as an intelligent person with the ability to understand the options available to you and the ability to make your own decision based on the information provided to you?

Are you able to understand and easily communicate with the attorney? Is he speaking to you in plain English or is his explanation of the matter so full of legalese to be almost meaningless?

Do you find the attorney's personality to be pleasant or grating? Sometimes people rub each other the wrong way. It is like rubbing a cat the wrong way. Stroking a cat from head to tail is pleasing to the cat, but petting it in the opposite direction, no matter how well intended, causes friction. If the lawyer makes you feel annoyed or uncomfortable, then find another attorney.

It is worth the effort to take the time to interview as many attorneys as it takes to find one with the right expertise, fee schedule and personality for you.

The First Week

Dealing with the death of a close family member or friend is difficult. Not only do you need to deal with your own emotions, but often with those of your family and friends. Sometimes their sorrow is more painful to you than what you are experiencing yourself.

In addition to the emotional impact of a death, there are many things that need to be done, from arranging the funeral and burial, to closing out the business affairs of the *decedent* (the person who died) and finally giving whatever property is left to the proper beneficiary.

The funeral and burial take only a few days. Wrapping up the affairs of the decedent may take considerably longer. This chapter explains what things you (the spouse or closest family member) need to do during the first week, beginning at the moment of death and continuing through the funeral.

 MALE GENDER USED

Rather than use "he/she" or "his/her" for simplicity
(and hoping not to offend anyone)
we will refer to the decedent and his
Personal Representative using the male gender.

References to other people will be in both genders.

In January 1, 2000, California's **Domestic Partner** laws went into effect. The statute gave a couple, each 18 or older, the right to become Domestic Partners by filling out a DECLARATION OF DOMESTIC PARTNER form obtained from the County Clerk. Once the couple completes the form and pays the filing fee, the Declaration is filed with the Secretary of State who then enters the Declaration in a Domestic Partnerships Registry. The Domestic Partner registration enables couples of the same sex to publicly proclaim their union.

Recognizing that there are elderly people who do not want to jeopardize their Social Security or widow(er) pension by marrying, the statute extended the Domestic Partner registration to heterosexual couples over the age of 62.

Initially, the statute provided few rights or responsibilities for the couple, however as of January 1, 2005, section 297.5 of the Family Code is amended to read:

> Registered domestic partners shall have the same rights, protections, and benefits, and shall be subject to the same responsibilities, obligations, and duties under law, whether they derive from statutes, administrative regulations, county rules, government policies, common law, or any other provision or sources of law, as are granted to and imposed upon spouses.

Registered Domestic Partners now have the same rights and responsibilities as a spouse within the state of California. We will use the designation "Spouse/RDP" to indicate that the quoted law applies to the decedent's spouse or his Registered Domestic Partner

NOTE ⇨ CALIFORNIA'S DOMESTIC PARTNER STATUTES DO NOT APPLY TO OTHER STATES OR TO THE FEDERAL GOVERNMENT

The Domestic Partner designation is unique to the state of California. The federal government does not recognize the relationship and will consider Domestic Partners to be friends and not relatives. Other states, may or may not, recognize the relationship depending on their state law. Most states have laws that prohibit recognition of a same sex union.

Other states allow limited rights for Domestic Partners. For example, Arizona statute allows a Domestic Partner to make an anatomical gift on behalf of the deceased partner, provided no one else has assumed financial responsibility for the decedent. In New Jersey, a Domestic Partner relationship is established by a couple who obtain a *Certificate of Domestic Partnership* from the New Jersey State Registrar. New Jersey will recognize a Domestic Partnership that is valid in another state, however, Domestic Partners in the state of New Jersey have only those rights and responsibilities as established by New Jersey law. See *Guiding Those Left Behind In New Jersey* by Amelia E. Pohl for a discussion of those rights and responsibilities.

AUTOPSIES

In today's high tech world of medicine, doctors are fairly certain of the cause of death, but if there is a question, the family should consider having an autopsy performed. The decedent may have appointed an Agent under a Power of Attorney For Health Care with power to authorize the autopsy (Probate 4683). If not, any one of the following can give permission for the examination:

⇨ Spouse/RDP
⇨ an adult child or a parent
⇨ a brother or sister
⇨ any other kinsfolk who has the right to control the disposition of the body
⇨ anyone who has the right to dispose of the remains
⇨ a public administrator or Coroner.

If the decedent was a member of a religion that relies solely upon prayer for healing, the authorization must be in writing (Health & Safety 7113).

The person who authorizes the autopsy must agree to pay for it because the cost of the examination is not covered under most health insurance plans. That cost could be sizeable, running anywhere from several hundred to several thousand dollars. Still, it may be in the family's best interest to consent to the autopsy. The examination might reveal a genetic disorder that could be treated if it later appears in another family member. Death from a car "accident" could have been a heart attack at the wheel. Perhaps the patient who died suddenly in a hospital was misdiagnosed. The nursing home resident could have died from negligence and not old age.

Even if none of these are found, knowing the cause of death with certainty is better than not knowing.

That was the case with the family of an elderly woman who was taken to the hospital complaining of stomach pains. The doctors thought she might be suffering from gallbladder disease but she died before they could effectively treat her. A doctor suggested that an autopsy be performed to determine the exact cause of death.

The woman had three daughters, one of whom objected to the autopsy: "Why spend that kind of money? It won't bring Mom back."

The daughter's wishes were respected, however over the years as they aged and became ill with their own various ailments, they would undergo physical examinations. As part of taking their medical history, doctors routinely asked "And what was the cause of your mother's death?"

None could answer the question.

This is not a dramatic story. No mysterious genetic disorder ever occurred in any of her daughters, nor in any of their children. But each daughter (including the one who objected) at some point in her life, was confronted with the nagging question "What did Mom die of?"

DEATH FROM NATURAL CAUSES

When a person dies, a physician, or the Coroner, must sign a medical statement identifying the cause of death. If a person dies in a hospital, there is someone present to sign. There is no need to call 911 if a person, who was gravely ill dies at home, provided he had been examined by a doctor within 20 days of the death (Gov't 27491). The funeral director will take possession of the body. He will have the treating physician sign the medical statement. The funeral director will file the certificate of death with the local Registrar of the Division of Vital Statistics (Gov't 27491.5).

A law enforcement officer must be summoned whenever a person dies suddenly and unexpectedly from illness, accident, suicide or foul play. In such case, the officer will ask the Coroner to determine the cause and manner of death. The Coroner will take charge of the body and make his investigation. He may have an autopsy performed if he suspects that the death was not from natural causes or that the death was caused by a disease that poses a threat to the public health (Gov't 27491).

Once the Coroner takes possession of a body, it will not be released until the examination is complete (Health & Safety 7102). Meanwhile, the family can proceed with arrangements for the funeral. The funeral director will contact the Coroner to determine when he can pick up the body and proceed with the burial or cremation.

MANDATORY AUTOPSIES

When a person dies, a physician must sign a medical certification stating the cause of death. This is not a problem if a person dies in a hospital or nursing home from natural causes. If he dies at home and the death was expected, the treating physician can be contacted to sign the medical certificate verifying that the decedent died of natural causes. But if a person dies, suddenly, at home and he was not under the care of a physician, whoever discovers the body must call 911 to summon the police. The law enforcement officer will call the Coroner to determine the cause of death.

If the Coroner suspects that the death was not from natural causes or if the decedent died from a disease that might pose a threat to the public health, the Coroner may decide to have an autopsy performed. The cost of the examination is paid by the county in which the autopsy was performed.

If, before beginning the procedure, the Coroner is informed that the decedent signed a *Certificate of Religious Belief* stating that any postmortem anatomical dissection would violate his religious convictions, the Coroner will postpone the examination until the Certificate is produced. If the Certificate is produced, but the Coroner finds an autopsy is necessary to investigate a crime or determine whether the death was a result of a public health hazard, he will petition the Superior Court for an order authorizing the autopsy (Gov't 27491.43).

THE OPTIONAL AUTOPSY

If the Coroner determines that an autopsy is not necessary, but the family wants to know the actual cause of death, they can ask the Coroner to conduct an autopsy. The Coroner will do so, provided whoever is the next of kin makes the request in writing and agrees to pay for the cost of the examination (Gov't 27520).

AUTOPSIES PERFORMED BY THE INSURANCE COMPANY

A company that issues disability insurance in the state of California is required to include a statement in the policy that the company has the right to perform an autopsy. (Insur. 10350.10). Most accident and life insurance policies contain the same provision.

The cost of the autopsy is paid by the insurance company, so it will not order an autopsy unless there is some important reason to do so, such as whether the cause of death is covered under that policy.

ANATOMICAL GIFTS

Hospital personnel determine whether a mortally ill patient is a candidate for an organ donation. Early on in the donor program those over 65 were not considered as suitable candidates. Today, however, the condition of the organ, and not the age, is the determining factor.

The federal government has established regional Organ Procurement Organizations throughout the United States to coordinate the donor program. There are Organ Procurement Organizations that service Northern California (The California Transplant Donor Network); North Central California (The Golden State Donor Services) Imperial and San Diego counties (Life Sharing Community Organ Donation) and Southern California (One Legacy). If it is determined that the patient is a candidate, the hospital will contact the local Organ Procurement Organization.

GIFT AUTHORIZED PRIOR TO DEATH
A California registry of organ donors called **DONATE LIFE CALIFORNIA** was established in the year 2006. If the decedent indicated a desire to be an organ donor on his driver's licence, he name is included on the Registry (Vehicle 12811) If, the decedent is not on the Registry, but he signed an *Organ Donor Card*, hospital personnel or the donor's doctor need to be made aware of the gift in quick proximity to the time of death. If the donation is medically acceptable, the gift will be made. No family member need give permission provided the hospital has a copy of the decedent's unrevoked donor card.

GIFT AUTHORIZED BY THE FAMILY
If it is determined that the decedent is a suitable donor, and a donor card is not on record, someone who is specially trained will approach the family to request permission for the donation.

California statute establishes an order of priority to authorize the donation:

1st the Agent authorized by the decedent under a Power of Attorney For Health Care to make such gift.

2nd the Spouse/RDP   3rd an adult son or daughter

4th either parent of the decedent

5th an adult brother or sister   6th a grandparent

7th the decedent's Guardian or Conservator who was appointed prior to the death.

If permission is obtained from a family member and there are others in the same or a higher priority, then an effort must be made to contact those people and make them aware of the proposed gift. A gift cannot be made if someone with the same or higher priority objects to the gift. For example, if the brother of the decedent agrees to the gift (5th in priority) and decedent's adult child objects (3rd in priority), no gift can be made. Similarly, the statute prohibits the gift if the decedent ever expressed his opposition to a donation (Health & Safety 7151).

AFTER THE DONATION

Once the donation is made the body is delivered to the funeral home and prepared for burial or cremation as directed by the family. The donation does not disfigure the body so there can be an open casket viewing if the family so wishes.

Some regional Organ Procurement Organizations have an aftercare program that includes a letter of condolence to the family and an expression of gratitude for the gift. For privacy reasons, the identity of the recipient of the gift is not disclosed, but on request from the family, the local Organ Procurement Organization will give the family basic demographic information about the donation, such as the age, sex, marital status, number of children and occupation of the recipient of the gift.

CAVEAT: Federal law prohibits payment for organ donations (42 U.S.C. 274 (e)). There is no ban on payments made to prepare organs or tissue for transplantation, nor is there any ban on charges made to transport bodies or body parts. Not-for-profit, as well as for-profit, companies have sprung up that are in the business of preparing and delivering body parts. These companies request donations from families — so they are not violating federal law by paying for the donation. The company prepares the body tissue or other parts of the donated body, and then distributes the parts throughout the United States to physicians, hospitals, research centers, etc. In many cases, the amount charged for preparation and transportation includes a sizable profit.

If a company or organization, other than your local Organ Procurement Organization, approaches you to make a donation, before agreeing you may want to learn about the company making the request.

What is the name of the company?
Where are their main headquarters located?
What is their primary business activity?
What is the name and job description of the person making the request?

DETERMINE THE END USE OF THE DONATION

You may want to ask what they intend to do with the tissue or body part. If it is being used for research, then what type of research? Where is the research being conducted? If it will be used for transplantation, then what agency (doctor, hospital) will receive the donation and where is that agency located?

Once you have this information you can make an informed decision as to whether you wish to make the donation to that organization.

GIFT FOR EDUCATION OR RESEARCH

Consider offering to release the body for the purpose of education or research in the event that the decedent signed a donor card, but was not an appropriate candidate for an organ donation. You can offer to release the body for study or research to a school of medicine at a university, such as:

University of California at San Diego   (858) 534-4536
School of Medicine
La Jolla, CA 92093

University of California, San Francisco   (415) 476-1981
State Curator for No. California
San Francisco, CA 94143

Western University of Health Sciences   (909) 469-5431
College of Osteopathic Medicine
Pomona, CA 91766

You will need to call the school within 24 hours of the death to determine whether they will accept the body. Some require preregistration the decedent prior to his death and will not accept a donation by the family.

Most schools will not accept bodies from those who weigh more than 300 pounds or have died from a contagious disease or from crushing injuries. The school may ask the family to pay for transportation of the body to the facility.

It usually takes 18 months to 2 years to complete the study or research project. Facilities differ on the method of disposition of the body. The University of California at San Diego and the University of California at San Francisco cremate the remains and scatter them at sea. Some institutions charge a fee for the disposition of the body so you need to ask what it will cost to make the donation.

THE FUNERAL

Approximately ten percent of deaths occur suddenly because of accident, suicide, foul play or undetected illness. But, in general, death occurs after a lengthy illness, with a common scenario being that of an aged person who dies after being ill for several months, if not years. In such case, family and friends are prepared for the happening. Expected or not, the first job is the disposition of the body.

THE PRENEED FUNERAL ARRANGEMENT

Increasingly, people are arranging, in advance, for their own funeral and burial. This makes it easier on the family both financially and emotionally. All the decisions have been made and there is no guessing what the decedent would have wanted.

If the decedent made provision for his burial, you should come across a cemetery deed or perhaps a certificate for a burial plot. If he made provision for his funeral, you should find a PRENEED AGREEMENT. You need to read the contract to determine what arrangements were made. If the Agreement was being paid by installment, contact the funeral director to determine whether it is paid in full.

If you cannot locate the Agreement, but you know the name of the funeral home, call and ask them to send you a copy. They are required by law to give you a copy of the Agreement (Bus. & Prof. 7685, 7745). If you believe the decedent purchased a funeral plan but you do not know the name of the funeral home, call the local funeral homes. Many local funeral homes are owned by national firms with computer capacity to identify people who have purchased a contract at any of their many locations.

Once you have possession of the Agreement, take it with you to the funeral home and go over the terms of the with the funeral director. Determine whether the contract was a fixed price agreement or whether there will be additional charges.

TAKING RESPONSIBILITY FOR THE DISPOSITION

California statute (Health & Safety 7100) gives an order of priority of those people who have the right, and the financial responsibility, to arrange for final disposition in the event the decedent did not make his own arrangements:

1st   AGENT UNDER POWER OF ATTORNEY FOR HEALTH CARE

The person appointed as Health Care Agent has the job of following directions given in a Power of Attorney regarding the decedent's final disposition. He is not personally liable to pay for the funeral unless he agrees to do so. If he makes decisions regarding the disposition, he will be liable for those costs, but only if there are no other funds available in the decedent's Estate.

2nd   SPOUSE OR REGISTERED DOMESTIC PARTNER

If the surviving spouse or Registered Domestic Partner ("Spouse/RDP") is competent to do so, (s)he is responsible to make arrangements and pay for the reasonable cost of the disposition.

3rd   CHILD(REN)

A majority of the decedent's children have the right and responsibility to pay for the disposition.

4th   PARENT(S)

Parent(s) are responsible to make arrangements and pay for the final disposition, provided they are competent to do so.

5th SIBLINGS

A majority of the decedent's adult siblings are fifth in line to arrange and pay for the disposition.

6th NEXT OF KIN

Whoever is **next of kin** as determined by California's LAW'S OF INTESTATE SUCCESSION is responsible for the final disposition. See Chapter 5 for an explanation of these Laws. If two or more have the same degree of kinship, a majority of them have the duty to make arrangements. Less than a majority may be responsible, provided they used reasonable efforts to contact the people with the same degree of kinship and are not aware of any objection to the arrangements made.

7th THE PUBLIC ADMINISTRATOR

A public administrator will take responsibility for the final disposition, but only if there are sufficient funds in the decedent's Estate to pay for the disposition (Health & Safety 7100). If there is not enough money in the decedent's Estate, each and every one who is responsible to dispose of the body is also responsible to pay for the final disposition (Health & Safety 7100(d)). If the responsible person refuses or neglects to act, whoever makes the funeral arrangements can sue each person who is legally responsible for three times the cost of the disposition (Health & Safety 7103 (c)).

If family refuses or neglects to act within ten days, the state can arrange for the final disposition, and then file misdemeanor charges against the responsible person. If convicted (s)he can spend up to one year in the county jail and/or a fine of $10,000 (Health & Safety 7103(b), 7105(b)). In addition, the responsible person can be billed for the money spent by the state for the final disposition (Health & Safety 7104, 7104.1).

MAKING FUNERAL ARRANGEMENTS

If the decedent died unexpectedly or without having made any prior funeral arrangements, then your first job is to choose a funeral director and make arrangements for the funeral or cremation. Most people choose the nearest or most conveniently located funeral home without comparison shopping. However, prices for these services can vary significantly from funeral home to funeral home. Savings can be had if you take the time to make a few phone calls.

Receiving price quotes by telephone is your right under Federal law. Federal Trade Commission ("FTC") Rule 453.2 (b)(1) requires a funeral director to give an accurate telephone quote of the price of his goods and services. Funeral homes are listed in the telephone directory under FUNERAL DIRECTORS. If you live in a small town, there may be only one or two listings. If such is the case, check out some funeral homes in the next largest city.

Funeral directors usually provide the following services:
➤ arrange for the transportation of the body
    to the funeral home and then to the burial site
➤ obtain a Permit For Disposition
➤ arrange for the embalming or cremation of the body
➤ arrange funeral and memorial services
    and the viewing of the body
➤ obtain information for the death certificate
    and submit it to the Registrar of Vital Statistics
➤ order copies of the death certificate for the family
➤ have memorial cards printed.

To compare prices you will need to determine:

✧ what is included in the price of a basic funeral plan

✧ whether you can expect any additional cost.

It may be necessary to have the body embalmed if you are going to have a viewing. Embalming is not necessary if you order a direct cremation or an immediate burial without a viewing. Federal Trade Commission Rule 453.5 prohibits the funeral home from charging an embalming fee unless you order the service. If the decedent did not own a burial space, then that cost must be included when making funeral arrangements.

PURCHASING THE CASKET

Funeral directors are required to give you a written price list stating the cost of each service to be provided and each item to be purchased (Bus. & Prof. 7685, 7685.2). You will find that the single most expensive item is the casket. Directors usually quote a range of prices for the casket, saying that you need to choose the casket at the time you contract for the funeral.

When selecting a casket you need to be aware that there may be a considerable mark-up in the price quoted by the funeral director. You do not need to go "sole source" when purchasing the casket. You can purchase the casket elsewhere and have it delivered to the funeral home to be used instead of the one offered by the funeral director. Funeral homes are required to accept caskets purchased elsewhere, and they may not charge a handling fee for accepting that casket. However, if the price list given to you by the funeral home states that the price of their casket includes a specific dollar amount for basic services, then the funeral director is allowed to add that dollar amount to the charge for his services in the event you purchase the casket elsewhere (FTC Rule 453.2, 453.4).

Caskets are not usually displayed for sale at a shopping mall, so most of us have no idea of the going price for a casket. With the advent of the Internet, you can learn all about the cost of any item, even a casket, by using your search engine to find a retail casket sales dealer. If you are not computer literate, you can locate the nearest retail casket sales outlet by looking in the yellow pages under CASKETS. You may need to look in the telephone directory for the nearest large city to find a listing. By making a call to a retail casket sales dealer, you will become knowledgeable in the price range of caskets. You can then decide what is a reasonable price for the product you seek.

The best time to do your comparison shopping is before you go to the funeral home to arrange for the funeral. Once you have determined what you should pay for the casket, it is only fair to give the funeral director the opportunity to meet that price. If you cannot reach a meeting of the minds, you can always order the casket from the retail sales dealer and have it delivered to the funeral home.

ON-LINE FUNERAL SERVICES

The Internet is changing the way the world does business, and the funeral industry is no exception. A growing number of mortuaries are offering live Webcasts of funerals and wakes for those who are unable to pay their respects in person.

There are Web sites where you can post an obituary. There are on-line memorial chat rooms as well as on-line eulogies and testimonials. There is even a Web site that offers a posthumous E-mail service which allows people to leave final messages for friends and relatives. You can locate these services using your favorite search engine and typing in "obituaries."

THE CREMATION

Increasingly people are opting for cremation. The ASSOCIATION OF CALIFORNIA CREMATIONISTS, reports that in the year 2003, 52.61% of who died in California were cremated. They project that in 2010, that percentage will exceed 65%. The reasons for choosing cremation are varied, but for the majority, it is a matter of finances. The cost of cremation is approximately one-sixth that of an ordinary funeral and burial. A major saving is the cost of the casket. No casket is necessary for the cremation and Federal law prohibits a Funeral Director from saying that a casket is required for a direct cremation (FTC Rule 453.3 (b)ii). You may need a suitable container to deliver the body to the crematory. After the cremation, you will need an urn for the ashes.

If you are having a memorial service in a place of worship and no viewing of the body before the cremation, consider contracting with a facility that does cremations only. Look in the telephone book under CREMATION SERVICES. You will also see cremation "societies" in the telephone book. Some are for-profit and others not-for-profit. You can also find advertisements for cremation services on the Internet. These cremation facilities provide much the same services as a funeral home but with one important exception — the cremation service does not provide any type of funeral service or public viewing of the body.

THE DECEDENT WITH A PACEMAKER
Cremating a body with a pacemaker or any radiation producing device can cause damage to the cremation chamber or to the person performing the cremation. If the decedent was wearing such electronic aid, it needs to be removed prior to the cremation.

Some veterinary hospitals are implanting used pacemakers into pets who are suffering from heart disease. If the decedent was an animal advocate, consider making a donation of the pacemaker to the hospital in his memory.

THE OVERWEIGHT DECEDENT

Cremation technology has kept up with the expanding waist line of our population. Most cremation services can accommodate a body weighing up to 400 pounds. But if the decedent is extremely obese, you need to check to see whether the cremation service has facilities large enough to handle the body. If you cannot locate a crematory that can accommodate the body, you will need to make burial arrangements.

DISPOSING OF THE CREMAINS

The decedent's **cremains** (cremated remains) can be kept in a container at home. If they are to be placed in a cemetery, you need to obtain an urn (i.e., a durable container) for the burial (Health & Safety 7054.6). You can purchase the urn from the funeral director or Crematory Service Director. Urns cost much less than caskets, but they can cost several hundred dollars. You may wish to do some comparison shopping by calling a retail sales casket dealer.

Many cemeteries have a separate building called a *columbarium*, which is especially designed to store urns. Some cemeteries allow the cremains of a family member to be placed in an occupied family plot or mausoleum If you wish to have the cremains placed in an occupied mausoleum or family plot, call the cemetery and ask them to explain their policy as it relates to the burial of urns in occupied sites.

SCATTERED AT SEA

The decedent may have expressed a desire to have his ashes scattered at sea. State law requires that aircraft used to scatter ashes be registered by the Federal Aviation Administration and boats so used be registered with the Department of Motor Vehicles (Bus. & Prof. 9742).

Federal law prohibits the ashes from being scattered any closer than three nautical miles from land, so you will need to arrange to have a boat or aircraft to carry the ashes out to sea (Title 40 Code of Federal Regulations ("CFR") Section 229.1).

Cremains can be scattered in a lake or stream provided such scattering is at least 500 yards from shoreline (Health & Safety 7117 (c)).

Before the cremains are scattered, a death certificate is filed and a Permit for Disposition must be obtained the local Registrar (Health & Safety 103050). Whoever scatters the ashes must, within ten days, file a statement with the Registrar identifying the place where the ashes were scattered (Health & Safety 7117 (b), 103055). The funeral director or cremation director will be able to assist you in seeing to it that these regulations are followed.

If the decedent is to be buried in another state, you will need to arrange for the transportation of the body to that state. You will need to obtain a *Burial* or *Removal Permit* from the local Registrar of the district where the death occurred (Health & Safety 7055). If services are to be held in California and in the other state, contact a local funeral director and he will make arrangements with the out-of-state funeral home for the transportation of the body.

If you do not plan to have services conducted in California, you can contact the out-of-state funeral director and ask him to effect the transfer. Many funeral homes belong to a national network of funeral homes, so both the local and the out-of-state funeral director usually have the means to make arrangements to transport the body.

TRANSPORTING CREMAINS

If the body has been cremated, you can transport the cremains yourself, either by carrying the ashes as part of your luggage or by arranging with the airline to transport the ashes as cargo. Have a certified copy of the death certificate ready in the event that you need to identify the cremains of the decedent. You will also need a Burial or Removal Permit giving you authority to take the cremains out of state.

In these days of heightened security, it is important to call the airline before departure and ask whether they have any special regulation or procedure regarding the transportation of human ashes.

| SPOUSE | THE MILITARY BURIAL |

Subject to availability of burial spaces, an honorably discharged veteran and/or his unmarried minor or handicapped child and/or his un-remarried spouse may be buried in a national military cemetery.

The following cemeteries have room only for cremated remains or for the casketed remains of a family member of someone who is currently buried in that cemetery:

Fort Rosecrans National Cemetery   (619) 553-2084
San Diego, CA 92106

Golden Gate National Cemetery   (650) 761-1646
San Bruno, CA   94066

Los Angeles National Cemetery   (310) 268-4494
Los Angeles, CA 90049

San Francisco National Cemetery   (650) 761-1646
San Francisco, CA 94120

There is burial space available at the following National Cemeteries:

Riverside National Cemetery   (951) 653-8417
Riverside, CA 92518

San Joaquin Valley National Cemetery   (209) 854-1040
Gustine, CA 95322

Sacramento Valley VA National Cemetery   (707) 693-2460
Dixon, CA   95620

ARLINGTON NATIONAL CEMETERY

An honorably discharged veteran can be buried in the national military cemetery at Arlington, Virginia. The Department of the Army is in charge of the Arlington National Cemetery. You can call the Interment Service Branch at (703) 607-8585 for information about having a veteran buried there.

THE COST OF A MILITARY BURIAL

Burial space in a National Cemetery is free of charge. Cemetery employees will open and close the grave and mark it with a headstone or grave marker without cost to the family. If requested, the local Veteran's Administration ("VA") will provide the family with a memorial flag. The VA will not pay to have the body transported to the cemetery, so the family needs to make arrangements with a funeral firm to transport the remains to the cemetery.

Regardless of where an honorably discharged veteran is buried, allowances may be available for the plot, and the burial and grave marker expenses. The amount varies depending on factors such as whether the veteran died because of a service related injury. The VA will not reimburse any burial or funeral expense for the spouse of a veteran. For information about reimbursement of funeral and burial expenses you can call the VA at (800) 827-1000.

The Department of Veteran's Affairs has a Website with information on the following topics:

 ➢ National and Military Cemeteries
 ➢ Burial, Headstones and Markers
 ➢ State Cemetery Grants Program
 ➢ Obtaining Military Records
 ➢ Locating Veterans

VA CEMETERY WEB SITE
http://www.cem.va.gov

SPOUSE BENEFITS FOR SPOUSE OF DECEASED VETERAN

The surviving spouse of an honorably discharged veteran should contact the Veteran's Administration to determine whether he/she is eligible for any benefits. For example, if the decedent had minor or disabled children, his spouse may also be eligible for a monthly benefit of Dependency and Indemnity Compensation ("DIC").

Whether a surviving spouse is eligible for benefits depends on many factors, including whether the decedent was serving on active duty, whether his death was service related, and the amount of the surviving spouse's assets and income. DIC benefits are discontinued should the surviving spouse remarry; however, the law allows payments to be reinstated in the event that the subsequent marriage ends because of death or divorce.

For information about whether the surviving spouse is eligible for any benefit related to the decedent's military service call the VA at (800) 827-1000.

You can receive a printed statement of public policy: VA Pamphlet 051-000-00228-8 FEDERAL BENEFITS FOR VETERANS AND DEPENDENTS by sending a $7 check to:
THE SUPERINTENDENT OF DOCUMENTS
P.O. Box 371954
Pittsburgh, PA 15250-7954
Or you can download it without charge from the Internet.

 VETERAN'S ADMINISTRATION
http://www.va.gov

 **LAWYER** THE WRONGFUL DEATH

It is important to have a Personal Injury attorney investigate any accidental death, to determine whether the death was caused by the wrongful act of a person, or company. If the accident was related to the decedent's job, the family may wish to consult with a Worker's Compensation attorney as well.

California statute (Civ. Proc. 377.60) restricts those who can sue for the *wrongful death* of the decedent to his Spouse/RDP and *lineal descendants* (child, grandchild, etc.). If there are no lineal descendants, those who are entitled to inherit through California's LAWS OF INTESTATE SUCCESSION have the right to sue. Those laws are discussed in Chapter 5. Whoever intentionally killed the decedent may not profit from that act, so he may not sue for a wrongful death. In such case, the person who may bring an action for wrongful death is determined as if the killer died before the decedent (Probate 258).

In general, the person who is suing is entitled to economic losses suffered, but there may be limits to the amount compensation for *non-economic damages* such as physical impairment, disfigurement, inconvenience, pain and suffering. If the wrongful death was caused by the negligence of a health care provider (doctor, nurse, hospital, etc.) non-economic damages are limited to $250,000. If the decedent was in an automobile accident and he was driving without insurance, or "under the influence," his Estate is not entitled to recover for non-economic damages (Civil 3333.2, 3333.4).

| Special Situation | VICTIMS OF CRIME COMPENSATION PROGRAM |

The State of California reimburses crime victims who suffer losses that are not covered by insurance or any other compensation. If a the decedent died because of a criminal act, a *derivative victim*, i.e., someone who suffers a loss because of the crime has the right to be compensated for economic losses he suffered. Depending on the relation of the derivative victim to the decedent, compensation may be paid for lost income, mental health counseling, funeral expenses, etc. Total compensation paid to all victims may not exceed $70,000 (Gov't 13957.5, 13957).

The award process may take up to three months, but if emergency funds are needed (for example, to pay for the burial), they can release up to $1,500. Emergency funds will be deducted from the final award (code).

The **California Victim Compensation and Government Claims Board** administers the program (Gov't 13951). To be eligible, the following must be true:

➢ There was full cooperation with law enforcement officers by the decedent and derivative victim.

➢ The decedent and the derivative victim was innocent of the crime (Gov't 13956).

To file a claim you can call the Board (800) 777-9229 or you can download a Crime Victim Compensation Application from the State Board of Control Web site.

STATE BOARD OF CONTROL
http://www.boc.ca.gov/Victims

Police make every effort to identify and locate the family of an unclaimed body. The Coroner will arrange for the burial or cremation of any body that is unidentified or unclaimed. The Coroner may make an anatomical gift upon request from an Organ Procurement Organization (Health & Safety 7155.7). If no request is made the Coroner will contact the State department and offer to donate the body to a school of medicine in California for the purpose of education or scientific research (Health & Safety 7203). The Coroner will not make such donation if he learns that such donation was against the decedent's religious belief (Gov't 27491.43).

Whenever an inmate of any state correctional institution dies, the Director of Corrections, or other person in charge, will notify the relative of the decedent. If no relative can be found, or if no one will take responsibility for the disposition of the body, he will arrange for the burial or cremation of the body (Penal 5061).

THE INDIGENT VETERAN

As explained previously, an honorably discharged veteran can be buried without charge — with the exception of transportation costs to the veteran's cemetery.

| Special
Situation | THE PROBLEM
FUNERAL OR BURIAL |

The funeral and burial industry is well regulated by the state and federal government. Under California law the following acts are subject to disciplinary action:

☒ Neglecting to furnish the customer with a written price list at the beginning of the discussion (Bus. & Prof. 7685, 7685.2).

☒ Using a false or misleading advertisement (Bus. & Prof. 7693).

☒ Paying "steerer" or "solicitors" to generate business (Bus. & Prof. 7695, 7701).

☒ Using profane, indecent or obscene language in the presence of the body or a family member (Bus. & Prof. 7700)

Funeral directors are licensed professionals so it is unusual to have a problem with the funeral or burial or cremation. If, however, you had a bad experience with any aspect of the funeral, you can file a complaint with the **CALIFORNIA DEPARTMENT OF CONSUMER AFFAIRS** at (800) 952-5210, or call the Cemetery and Funeral licensing agency at (916) 574-7870, or write to them at:

Cemetery and Funeral Bureau
1625 N. Market Blvd., Ste S208
Sacramento, CA 95834

 In addition to filing a complaint with the Board, you may wish to consult with an attorney who is experienced in litigation matters to learn of any other legal remedy that you may have.

Few things are more difficult to deal with than a missing person. The emotional turmoil created by the "not knowing" is often more difficult than the finality of death. The legal problems created by the disappearance are also more difficult than if the person simply died. It may take a three-part legal process — the appointment of a *Conservator* to handle the missing person's affairs during his absence, having a hearing to determine whether to presumed that he is dead, and if so, a Probate proceeding to settle his affairs.

APPOINTING A CONSERVATOR

An **Absentee** is a person who is missing and cannot be found after a diligent search. If the Absentee has business matters that need attending (bills that need to be paid, family to be supported), his next of kin can ask the Court to appoint a Conservator who will manage the property, under Court supervision, until the Absentee can be found (Probate 1849, 1849.5, 1850). You need to consult with an experienced Probate attorney, to have the Conservator appointed.

BEGINNING THE PROBATE PROCEDURE

A Probate procedure any time there is sufficient evidence that the Absentee is dead, or after the Absentee has been missing for five years (Probate 12401). The judge will hear evidence to determine whether the missing person should be presumed dead; and if so, the Probate procedure can go forward (Probate 12406). Should the missing person turn up after his property has been distributed, he has the right to reclaim his property (Probate 12408).

THE DEATH CERTIFICATE

It is the job of the funeral director to provide information about the death to the local Registrar of Vital Statistics. The Office of Vital Statistics will prepare a death certificate based on that information. It is important that the information you give to the funeral or cremation director is correct. You need to check the form completed by the funeral director to be sure names are correctly spelled and dates correctly written. Once the information is sent to Vital Statistics, it will be difficult and time consuming to make a correction.

The funeral director will order as many certified copies of the death certificate as you request. Most establishments require an original certified copy and not a photocopy so you need to order sufficient certified copies. The following is a list of institutions that may request a certified copy:

* Each insurance company that insured the decedent or his property (health insurance, life insurance, car insurance, etc.)
* Each financial institution in which the decedent had money invested (brokerage houses, banks)
* The decedent's pension fund
* Each credit card company used by the decedent
* The Internal Revenue Service
* The Social Security Administration
* The Department of Motor Vehicles
* If Probate is necessary, the Clerk of the Superior Court
* The County Recorder in each county where the decedent owned real property.

Some airlines and car rental companies offer a discount for short notice, emergency trips. If you have family flying in for the funeral, you may wish to order a few extra copies of the death certificate so that they can obtain an airline or car rental discount.

CERTIFIED COPIES ARE RESTRICTED
In an effort to stop the illegal use of birth and death certificates and reduce identity theft, the California legislature passed a law restricting the issuance of certified copies of these records. A certified copy of the birth or death certificate of the decedent will be issued only to the following people:

⇨ the Spouse/RDP, child, sibling, grandparent, grandchild

⇨ the parent or legal Guardian

⇨ the party entitled to receive the record as a result of a Court order

⇨ a member of law enforcement or other governmental agency conducting official business

⇨ the personal appointed by the Court to settle his Estate or his attorney

⇨ the funeral director or his employee (Health & Safety 103526).

If you need a certified copy of the death certificate at a later date, you can call the funeral director for additional copies, or if you are any of the above, you can order copies yourself.

VIA THE INTERNET

You can order the death certificate from the Web site of the Department of Health Services.

 DEPARTMENT OF HEALTH SERVICES
http://www.dhs.ca.gov/

FROM THE COUNTY RECORDER

Death records for the current year and the prior year are available from the County Recorder. You can find the address and telephone numbers of the office of the County Recorder at the above Web site. You can go to the Recorder's Office in the county where the death occurred and obtain a death certificate. This the fastest way to get the death certificate.

BY MAIL

You can obtain a certified copy of the death certificate by writing to: California Department Of Health Services
Office of Vital Records — M.S. 5103
P.O. Box 997410
Sacramento, CA 95899-7410

It is a good idea to first call the CUSTOMER SERVICE UNIT at (916) 445-2684 (Monday through Friday, 8 a.m. to 12 noon Pacific Standard Time) to check cost and procedure for ordering a death certificate.

It may take several weeks before you receive the death certificate, so you may want to ask them about the cost of getting the document by priority mail.

About Probate

Once a person dies, all of the property he owns as of the date of his death is referred to as the *decedent's Estate.* If the decedent owned property in his name only, with no provision for the automatic transfer of the property upon his death, then some sort of court procedure may be necessary to determine who now owns that property. The name of the court procedure is *Probate*. In California, Probate is conducted in the Probate section of the Superior Court (Probate 7050). We will use the term Court" or "Probate Court" to refer to the judge who is presiding over Probate matters.

The root of the word Probate is "to prove." It refers to the first job of the Probate Court, that is, to examine proof of whether the decedent left a valid Will. The second job of the Court is to appoint someone to wrap up the affairs of the decedent by paying the cost of the Probate procedure, any outstanding bills, and then distributing whatever is left to the proper beneficiary.

If the decedent left a valid Will naming someone as *Executor* of his Estate, the Court will appoint that person for the job and issue *Letters Testamentary* giving him authority to administer the Estate. If the decedent died without a Will, the Court will appoint someone to be the *Administrator* of his Estate and issue *Letters of Administration.* For simplicity we will refer to the person appointed by the court to settle the decedent's Estate as the *Personal Representative*, and the document authorizing him to act, as *Letters* (Probate 52).

There are different ways to conduct a Probate procedure depending on the value of the property that is being Probated, and whether the decedent owned real property at the time of his death. We will refer to the property that is distributed as part of a Probate procedure as the decedent's **Probate Estate** and the method of conducting the Probate as the **Estate Administration**.

Chapter 6 explains the different kinds of Estate Administration that are available in the state of California.

But we are getting ahead of ourselves. First we need to determine whether a Probate procedure is necessary. To answer that question we need to know exactly what the decedent owned, so the next two chapters explain how to identify, and then locate, the decedent's assets.

Giving Notice Of The Death 2

Those closest to the decedent usually notify family members and close friends by telephone. The funeral director will arrange to have an obituary published in as many different newspapers as the family requests, but there is still the job of notifying the government and people who were doing business with the decedent. That is the responsibility of the person appointed as Personal Representative of the decedent's Estate.

California law gives an order of priority for the appointment of Personal Representative. Whoever the decedent named as Executor or Personal Representative in his Will has top priority. Once appointed, it is his job to give notice of the death.

If the decedent died *intestate*, i.e., without a valid Will, the surviving Spouse/RDP has priority to be appointed as Personal Representative, so it is up to the Spouse/RDP to let everyone know of the death (Probate 8461). If there is no Spouse/RDP, the job falls to his next of kin. By *next of kin,* we mean those people who inherit the decedent's property according to California's LAWS OF INTESTATE SUCCESSION. Those laws are explained in Chapter 5.

The person who has the job of settling the decedent's Estate should begin to give notice as soon as is practicable after the death. Two government agencies that need to be notified are the Social Security Administration and the IRS. This chapter explains how to notify these and other agencies of the death.

Some funeral directors will, as part of their service package, notify the Social Security Administration of the death. You may wish to check to see that this has been done. You can do so by calling (800) 772-1213. If you are hearing impaired call (800) 325-0778 TTY. You will need to give the Social Security Administration the full legal name of the decedent as well as his Social Security number and date of birth.

Special Situation — DECEDENT RECEIVING SOCIAL SECURITY

If the decedent was receiving checks from Social Security, you need to determine whether his last check needs to be returned to the Social Security Administration. Each Social Security check is a payment for the prior month, provided that person lives for the entire prior month. If the decedent died on the last day of the month, you should not cash the check for that month.

For example, if he died on July 31st, you need to return the Social Security check mailed in August. If however, he died on August 1st the check sent in August does not need to be returned because it was payment for the month of July.

If the Social Security check is electronically deposited into a bank account, notify the bank and the Social Security Administration that the account holder died. If the check needs to be returned, the Social Security Administration will withdraw it electronically from the bank account. You will need to keep the account open until the funds are withdrawn.

SPOUSE/CHILD'S SOCIAL SECURITY BENEFITS

SPOUSE

If the decedent had sufficient work credits, the Social Security Administration will give the decedent's surviving spouse, or if unmarried, his minor child, a one-time death benefit in the amount of $255.

SURVIVORS BENEFITS:

The spouse (or former spouse) of the decedent may be eligible for Survivors Benefits. Benefits vary depending on the amount of work credits earned by the decedent; whether the decedent had minor or disabled children; the spouse's age; how long they were married; etc. The minor child of the decedent may be eligible for benefits regardless of whether the child's father (the decedent) ever married the child's mother. Paternity can be established by any one of several methods including the father acknowledging his child, in writing or verbally, to members of his family. You can also get information and download publications that explain survivors benefits from the Social Security Web site.

SOCIAL SECURITY ADMINISTRATION
http://www.socialsecurity.gov

SOCIAL SECURITY BENEFITS

A surviving spouse, or former spouse, can collect Social Security benefits based on the decedent's work record. This value may be greater than the amount the surviving spouse now receives. It is important to call (800) 772-1213 and make an appointment with your local Social Security office to determine whether you, as the surviving, or former spouse, are eligible for Social Security or Survivor benefits.

DECEDENT WITH GOVERNMENT PENSION

Any pension or annuity check received after the date of death of a federal retiree, or a survivor annuitant, needs to be returned to the U.S. Treasury. If the check is direct deposited to a bank account, call the financial institution and ask them to return the check. If the check is sent by mail, you need to return it to the return mail address on the Department of Treasury envelope in which the check was mailed. Include a letter explaining the reason for the return of the check and stating the decedent's date of death.

$$$ APPLY FOR BENEFITS $$$

A survivor annuity may be available to a surviving spouse, and/or minor or disabled child. In some cases, a former spouse may be eligible for benefits. Even though you notify the government of the death, they will not automatically give you benefits to which you may be entitled. You need to apply for those benefits by notifying the Office of Personnel Management ("OPM") of the death and requesting that they send you an application for survivor benefits. You can call them at (888) 767-6738 or you can write to:

U S. OFFICE OF PERSONNEL MANAGEMENT
RETIREMENT OPERATIONS CENTER
Post Office Box 45
Boyers, PA 16017

You will find brochures and information about Survivor's Benefits at the OPM Website.

 OFFICE OF PERSONNEL MANAGEMENT
http://www.opm.gov

In most cases, pension and annuity checks are payment for the prior month. If the decedent received his pension or annuity check before his death, then no monies need be returned. Pension checks and/or annuity checks received after the date of death may need to be returned to the company. You need to notify the company of the death to determine the status of the last check sent to the decedent.

Before notifying the company, locate the policy or pension statement that is the basis of the income. That document should tell whether there is a beneficiary of the pension or annuity funds now that the pensioner or annuitant is dead. If you cannot locate the document, use the return address on the check envelope and ask the company to send you a copy of the plan. Also request that they forward to you any claim form that may be required in order for the survivor or beneficiary to receive benefits under that pension plan or policy.

If the pension/annuity check is direct deposited to the decedent's account, ask the bank to assist you in locating the company and notifying the company of the death.

NOTIFYING IRS

The surviving spouse can file a final joint federal and state income tax return. A Registered Domestic Partner cannot file a joint federal income tax return, however (s)he can elect to file a joint state return. If a Personal Representative is appointed, he will need to sign the joint return as well (Rev. & Tax 18521). If there is no surviving Spouse/RDP, whoever is appointed as Personal Representative will have authority to file the final return. The decedent's final federal income tax return (IRS form 1040) needs to be filed by April 15th of the year following the year in which he died. If the decedent earned income in California in the year that he died, a state income tax return must be filed at the same time (Rev. & Tax 18566).

The California income tax return is filed with the California FRANCHISE TAX BOARD (Rev. & Tax 17041). You can get information about how to file the final California return by calling (800) 852-5711. Out of state, call (916) 845-6600. You can also get information from the Franchise Tax Board Web site.

FRANCHISE TAX BOARD
http://www.ftb.ca.gov

You may want to keep the decedent's bank account open until you determine whether the decedent is entitled to an income tax refund. See Chapter 6 for an explanation of how to obtain a tax refund.

THE GOOD NEWS
Monies inherited from the decedent do not count as income to you, so you do not pay income tax on those monies. If the money you inherit later earns interest or income, then of course you need to report that income the same as any other income.

AN ESTATE TAX FOR THE WEALTHY

Both the federal and state government have the right to impose an *Estate Tax* on property transferred to a beneficiary as a result of the death. All the property owned as of the date of death becomes the decedent's *Taxable Estate.* This includes *real property* (residential lots, condominiums etc.) and *personal property* (life insurance policies, cars, business interests, securities, IRAs, etc.). It includes property held in the decedent's name alone, as well as property that he held jointly or in Trust. It also includes gifts given by the decedent during his lifetime that exceeded the *Annual Gift Tax Exclusion.* That value was $10,000 per person, per year until 2002 when it was adjusted for inflation to $11,000 and again in 2006 to $12,000 (26 U.S.C. 2503(b)). For most of us, this is not a concern because no federal Estate Tax need be paid unless the decedent's Taxable Estate exceeds the federal *Estate Tax Exclusion Amount*. That value is currently two million dollars and is scheduled to go even higher:

YEAR	ESTATE TAX EXCLUSION AMOUNT
2007-2008	$2,000,000
2009	$3,500,000

Under current law, the federal Estate Tax is scheduled to be phased out in the year 2010, but reinstated once again in the year 2011 with an Exclusion Amount of $1,000,000 — unless lawmakers change the tax law once again.

There is an unlimited marital deduction for property transferred to the surviving spouse who is a U.S. citizen; so in most cases, no Estate tax need be paid if the decedent was married. Regardless of whether taxes are due, federal and state Estate Tax returns must be filed whenever the decedent's Estate exceeds the federal Estate Tax Exclusion Amount in effect as of his date of death. The federal return is due within nine months of the date of death (26 U.S.C. 6075).

THE CALIFORNIA "PICK-UP" ESTATE TAX

The California Estate Tax is based on the federal Estate Tax. The federal government imposes a tax on all property transferred because of the death, with certain exceptions for transfers made to a U.S. citizen spouse and to qualified charities. The federal government then grants an Estate Tax exclusion so that no federal Estate Tax need be paid unless the amount transferred at death is greater than the federal Estate Tax Exclusion amount. See the prior page for the current value of the Estate Tax Exclusion amount.

The California Estate Tax is called a "pick-up" tax, because the state collects the tax that would have gone to the federal government had it not been for a credit allowed on the federal Estate Tax return for death taxes paid to the state (Rev. & Tax 13302).

The Economic Growth and Tax Relief Reconciliation Act of 2001 amended the Internal Revenue Code to provide that an Estate cannot claim a credit for state death taxes for those who die after December 31, 2004. Because no credit is allowed for state death taxes on the federal Estate Tax return, there is no California Estate Tax for the years 2005 through 2010.

In the year 2011, and beyond, the federal Estate Tax exclusion is scheduled to be $1,000,000, with the state credit for federal Estate Tax restored. If there are no changes to the law, California will, once again collect a portion of the federal Estate Tax.

THE UN-UNIFIED GIFT TAX

As explained, the federal Annual Gift Tax Exclusion was $10,000 up until 2002. It is $12,000 for the year 2006. The IRS keeps a running count of amounts you give to someone that exceed the Annual Gift Tax Exclusion that is in effect in the year of your donation. Although you are required to report a gift that exceeds the Annual Gift Tax Exclusion, no tax needs to be paid unless your running count is more than the federal lifetime Gift Tax Exclusion. That amount is currently one million dollars.

If your running total does not exceed your lifetime Gift Tax Exclusion Amount, once you die, the value of the gifts reported to the IRS will be added to your Taxable Estate for Estate Tax purposes. If you are in that tax bracket, your beneficiaries may need to pay an Estate Tax on gifts made during your lifetime.

Until the Estate Tax law was changed, the Gift and Estate Tax were unified. No Gift Tax needed to be paid unless the total value of the taxable gifts exceeded the federal Estate Tax Exclusion Amount. In 2004 that changed. The Estate Tax Exclusion amount went up to $1,500,000, but the amount for the Gift Tax Exclusion remained at $1,000,000, so they now are no longer unified.

To summarize:
If you make a gift to anyone greater than the Annual Gift Tax Exclusion for that year, you must report the gift to the IRS. The IRS keeps a running count of gifts you made in excess of the Annual Gift Tax Exclusion. You will pay a Gift Tax on gifts given during your lifetime in excess of one million dollars. If the running count does not exceed one million dollars, it is added to your Taxable Estate once you die. The Estate Tax is scheduled to be phased out in 2010, but not the federal Gift Tax.

The current federal Estate tax is scheduled to be phased out in the year 2010, but a new Capital Gains Tax is scheduled for 2010 that may prove even more costly than the Estate Tax. The new Capital Gains Tax is related to the way inherited property is evaluated by the federal government. Real and personal property is inherited at a "stepped-up" basis, meaning that if the decedent's property increased in value from the time he acquired it, the beneficiary inherits the property at its fair market value as of the decedent's date of death.

For example, if the decedent bought stock for $20,000 and it is worth $50,000 as of his date of death, the beneficiary will take a step-up in basis of $30,000; i.e. the beneficiary inherits the stock at the current $50,000 value. If the beneficiary sells the stock for $50,000, he pays no Capital Gains Tax. If the beneficiary holds onto the stock and later sells it for $60,000, the beneficiary will pay a Capital Gains Tax only on the $10,000 increase in value since the decedent's death.

Up to 2009, there is no limit to the amount a beneficiary can take as a step-up in basis. But in 2010 caps are set in place. The decedent's Estate will be allowed a 1.3 million dollar step-up in basis, plus another 3 million for property passing to the surviving spouse (26 U.S.C. 1022(b)).

The new law could result in significant Capital Gains Taxes that the beneficiary must pay. For example, suppose in 2010 you inherit a business from your father that he purchased for $100,000 and it is now worth 2 million dollars. There is a capital gain of 1.9 million dollars, but you are allowed a step-up in basis of only 1.3 million. If you sell it for 2 million dollars $600,000 of your inheritance will be subject to a Capital Gains Tax.

SPOUSE ➤ SELLING THE HOME

In the tough "ol' days" the IRS allowed *Capital Gains Tax Exclusion* (up to $125,000) on the sale of one's **homestead** (i.e., principal residence). A person had to be 55 or older to take advantage of the Capital Gains Tax Exclusion, and it was a once-in-a-lifetime tax break. If a married couple sold their home and took the Tax Exclusion it was "used up" and no longer available to either partner.

In these, the good times, the IRS allows you to sell your home and up to $250,000 ($500,000 for a married couple) of the profit is free of the Capital Gains Tax. There is no limit to the number of times you can use the Exclusion, provided you own and live in the home at least two of the last five years prior to the sale (26 U.S.C. 121).

If, under the old law, the decedent and his spouse used their "once in a lifetime" Capital Gains Exclusion, with this new law, the surviving spouse can sell the homestead and once again take advantage of the tax break.

| Special Situation | BENEFICIARY OF THE CALIFORNIA HOMESTEAD |

The County Assessor must be notified of the change of ownership, if the decedent's homestead is transferred to a new owner through sale or inheritance. People who own a residence in California are entitled to a *Homeowners' Property Tax Exemption* provided they occupy the homestead as their primary residence. The Property Tax Exemption is currently (i.e., for the year 2007) $7000 of the value of the home (Rev. & Tax 218) . If the new owner is going to occupy the property as his homestead, he needs to apply to the County Assessor for his own Homestead Property Tax Exemption.

There are additional Property Tax Exemptions for disabled Veterans. If the decedent was a disabled Veteran, his surviving Spouse/RDP is eligible for the same Property Tax Exemption for so long as the Spouse/RDP does not remarry or enter into another RDP relationship. These exemptions apply to property owned together with the decedent or separate property held in the name of the surviving Spouse/RDP (Rev. & Tax 205.5).

The BOARD OF EQUALIZATION is an agency established to ensure that property taxes are applied uniformly throughout the state. You can get information about property taxes, as well as the telephone number and address of your local County Assessor, from the Board of Equalization Web site.

BOARD OF EQUALIZATION
http://www.boe.ca.gov

A decedent who was the **Settlor** (or *Grantor*) of a Trust, was probably managing the Trust as *Trustee* during his lifetime. The document that sets out the terms of the Trust (the **Trust Agreement)** should name a **Successor Trustee** to manage the Trust property now that the Settlor is deceased. The Trust Agreement may instruct the Successor Trustee to make certain gifts or the Agreement may direct the Successor Trustee to hold money in trust for a beneficiary of the Trust.

 **LAWYER**   IF YOU ARE
SUCCESSOR TRUSTEE

If you are the Successor Trustee, then in addition to following the terms of the Trust, you are required to obey all of the laws of the state of California relating to the administration of the Trust. For example, California statute requires the Successor Trustee to give a copy of the Trust to a beneficiary, or any heir of the decedent, who requests it (Probate 16061.5). The Successor Trustee has a duty to keep the beneficiaries of the Trust informed as to how the Trust is being administered (Probate 16060). You should consult with an attorney experienced in Estate Planning to help you administer the Trust according to the law and without any liability to you.

IF YOU ARE A BENEFICIARY OF THE TRUST

If you are a beneficiary of the Trust, you need to obtain a copy of the Trust to learn how the Trust will be administered now that the Settlor is deceased. Most Trust documents are written in "legalese," so you may want to employ your own attorney to review the Trust, and to explain your rights under the Trust.

NOTIFYING THE BUSINESS COMMUNITY

People and companies who were doing business with the decedent need to be notified of his death. This includes utility companies, credit card companies, brokerage firms, banks and companies that insured the decedent.

NOTIFY CREDIT CARD COMPANIES

You need to notify the decedent's credit card companies of the death. If you can find the contract with the credit card company, check to see whether the decedent had credit card insurance. If the decedent had credit card insurance, then the balance of the account is now paid in full. If you cannot find the contract, contact the company and get a copy of the contract along with a statement of the balance due as of the date of death.

DESTROY DECEDENT'S CREDIT CARDS

You need to destroy all of the decedent's credit cards. If you hold a credit card jointly with the decedent, then it is important to waste no time in closing that account and opening another in your name only.

That's something Barbara knows from hard experience. She and Hank never married but they did live together for several years before he died from liver disease. Hank came from a well to do family so he had enough money to support himself and Barbara during his long illness. Hank put Barbara on all of his credit card accounts so that she could purchase things when he became too ill to go shopping with her. After the funeral, Barbara had a gathering of friends and family at their apartment. Barbara was so preoccupied with her loss that she never noticed that Hank's credit cards were missing until the bills started coming in.

Barbara did not know who ran up the bills on Hank's credit cards during the month following his death. It was obvious that Hank's signature had been forged — but who forged it? One credit card company suspected that it might have been Barbara herself to get out of paying the bill by saying that the card had been stolen

Because the cards were held jointly, Barbara became liable to either pay the charges to the credit card or prove that she did not make the purchases. She was able to clear her credit record but it took several months and she had to employ an attorney to help her do so.

NOTIFY INSURANCE COMPANIES

Examine the decedent's financial records to determine the name and telephone number of all of the companies that insured the decedent or his property. This includes real property insurance, motor vehicle insurance, health insurance and life insurance.

MOTOR VEHICLE INSURANCE

Locate the insurance policy for any type of motor vehicle owed by the decedent (car, truck, boat, airplane) and notify the insurance company of the death. Determine how long insurance coverage continues after the death. Ask the insurance agent to explain what things are covered under the policy. Is the motor vehicle covered for all types of casualty (theft, accident, vandalism, etc.) or is coverage limited in some way?

If you can continue coverage, determine when the next insurance payment is due. Hopefully, the car will be sold or transferred to a beneficiary before that date, but if not, you need to arrange for sufficient insurance coverage during the Probate procedure.

LIFE INSURANCE COMPANIES

If the decedent's life was insured, you need to locate the policy and notify the company of his death. Call each life insurance company and ask what they require in order to forward the insurance proceeds to the beneficiary. Most companies will ask you to send them the original policy and a certified copy of the death certificate. Send the original policy by certified mail or any of the overnight services that require a signed receipt for the package. Make a copy of the original policy for your records before mailing the original policy to the company.

BANK ACCOUNT LIFE INSURANCE

Many banks, credit unions, and savings and loan associations provide life insurance at no cost to the owner of the account. While the amounts are generally small ($1,000 to $5,000), it is insurance that is often overlooked when settling the decedent's affairs. If you do not find a record of such policy, contact each financial institution to determine whether such insurance was offered to the decedent.

IF YOU CANNOT LOCATE THE POLICY

If you know that the decedent was insured, but you cannot locate the insurance policy, you can contact the company and request a copy of the policy. A tougher question is how to locate the policy if you do not know the name of the insurance company. The American Council of Life Insurers Web sit offers suggestions that you may find helpful.

AMERICAN COUNCIL OF LIFE INSURERS
http://www.acli.com

Go to the <u>Industry Products</u> section and then on to <u>Missing Policy.</u>

IF YOU CANNOT LOCATE THE COMPANY

If you cannot locate the insurance company it may be doing business under another name or it may no longer be doing business in the state of California. Each state has a branch of government that regulates insurance companies doing business in that state. If you are having difficulty locating the insurance company, you can call the Department of Insurance in the state where the policy was purchased and ask for assistance in locating the company. In California, you can call the Department of Insurance at (800) 927-4357. Out of state call (213) 897-8921. The Department of Insurance lists all of the insurance companies doing business in California at their Web site.

CALIFORNIA DEPARTMENT OF INSURANCE
http://www.insurance.ca.gov

EAGLE PUBLISHING COMPANY OF BOCA has the telephone number of the Department of Insurance for each state at the PUBLIC INFORMATION section of its Website.
http://www.eaglepublishing.com

WORK RELATED INSURANCE

If the decedent was employed, check his records for information about work related benefits. He may have survivor benefits from a company or group life insurance plan and/or a retirement plan. Also check with the employer about company benefits. If the decedent belonged to a union, ask the employer who you can contact to determine whether there are any union benefits.

The decedent may have belonged to a professional, fraternal or social organization such as the local Chamber of Commerce, a Veteran's organization, the Kiwanis, AARP, the Rotary Club, etc. If he belonged to any such organization, check to see whether the organization provided any type of insurance coverage.

 **BUSINESS OWNED BY DECEDENT**

If the decedent owned his own company or was a partner in a company, he may have purchased "key man" insurance. Key man insurance is a policy designed to protect the company should a valuable employee become disabled or die. Benefits are paid to the company to compensate the company for the loss of someone who is essential to the continuation of the business. Ultimately the policy benefits those who inherit the business.

If the decedent had an ownership interest in an ongoing business (sole proprietor, shareholder or partner), there may be a shareholder's or partnership agreement requiring the company to purchase the decedent's share of the business. The Personal Representative or his attorney needs to investigate to see if there was a key man insurance policy and/or such purchase agreement.

If the decedent was the sole owner of a corporation and the company stock was in his name only, there may need to be a Probate procedure before the company can be transferred to the new owner.

California statute requires each corporation to continuously maintain a *Designated Agent* in this state. If the decedent was the sole officer or Designated Agent of the company, the California Secretary of State needs to be notified of the identity of the new officers and Resident Agent as soon as is practicable (Corp. 1502, 1504).

Forms to change officers and Designated Agent can be obtained by calling (866) 275-2677 or you can download the form from the Internet.

 DEPARTMENT OF CORPORATIONS
http://www.corp.ca.gov

STATUS REPORT

If you were not actively involved in running the business, you might want to call the Department of Corporations or visit their Web site for a status report; i.e., the names, addresses of officers and directors, number of company shares, whether fees are current, etc.

HOMEOWNER'S INSURANCE

If the decedent owned his own home, check whether there is sufficient insurance coverage on the property. The decedent may have neglected to increase his insurance as the property appreciated in value. If so, it is important to increase coverage. If you think the property may be vacant for some period of time consider including vandalism coverage in the policy. Once the property is sold, or transferred to the proper beneficiary, you can have the policy discontinued or transferred to the new owner. The decedent's Estate should receive a refund for the unused portion of the premium.

MORTGAGE INSURANCE

If the decedent had a mortgage on any parcel of real estate that he owned, he might have arranged with his lender for an insurance policy that pays off the mortgage balance in the event of his death. Look at the closing statement to see whether there was a charge for mortgage insurance. Also check with the lender to determine if such a policy was purchased.

If there was no mortgage insurance, and the decedent was the sole owner, the beneficiary of the property needs to make arrangements with the lender to continue making payments on the mortgage or to refinance the loan.

NOTIFY THE HOMEOWNERS ASSOCIATION

If the decedent owned a condominium or a residence regulated by a homeowners association, the association will need to be notified of the change of ownership. Once the property is transferred, the new owner will need to contact the association to learn of the rules and regulations of the association. The new owner will need to arrange to have notices of dues and assessments forwarded to him.

HEALTH INSURANCE

You need to determine whether the decedent had health insurance, and if so, you should locate the original policy. If you know he had insurance, but cannot find the policy, have the insurance company send you a copy. The decedent's insurance carrier probably knows of the death, but it is a good idea to contact them to report the death and to verify that the medical treatment given before his death is covered by the policy.

 **DECEDENT ON MEDICARE**

If the decedent was covered by Medicare, you do not need to notify anyone, but you do need to know what things were covered by Medicare so that you can determine what medical bills are (or are not) covered by Medicare. The government publication **MEDICARE AND YOU** (Publication No. CMS-10050) explains what things are covered under Medicare and the different kinds of plans that are currently available. You can get the publication by writing to:

U.S. Dept. of Health and Human Services
Centers for Medicare and Medicaid Services
7500 Security Boulevard
Baltimore, MD 21244-1850

You can download the publication from the Internet.

 MEDICARE WEB SITE
http://www.medicare.gov

The publication is available on Audiotape, in Braille, in large print and in Spanish. Call (800) 633-4227 for a copy. TTY users call (877) 486-2048.

SPOUSE ▶ THE SPOUSE'S HEALTH INSURANCE

If the surviving spouse is insured under Medicare, the decedent's death does not affect the spouse's coverage. If the surviving spouse has her own health insurance plan that also covered the decedent, the spouse needs to notify the employer of the death because this may affect the cost of the plan to the employer and/or the surviving spouse. If the spouse was covered under the decedent's policy, (s)he needs to arrange for new coverage. There are state and federal laws that ensure continued coverage under the decedent's health insurance plan for a period of time depending on whether the decedent's employer falls under federal or state regulation.

If the decedent was employed by a federally regulated company (usually a company with at least twenty employees), under the Consolidated Omnibus Budget Reconciliation Act ("COBRA") the employer must make the company health plan available to the surviving spouse and any dependent child of the decedent for up to 36 months. The employer is required to give notice to the surviving spouse that the spouse and/or dependent child have the right to continue coverage under the decedent's health plan.

The spouse and/or child have 60 days from the date of death or 60 days after the employer sends notice (whichever is later) to tell the employer whether the surviving spouse and child wish to continue with the health insurance plan (29 U.S.C. Sec. 1162, 1163, 1165).

NO GRACE PERIOD FOR PAYMENT

Health Insurance premiums must be paid on or before each due date. If you wish continued coverage, you need to make that payment when it comes due.

A problem with continued coverage may be the cost. Before the death, the employer may have been paying some percentage of the premium. The employer has no such duty after the death unless there was some employment agreement stating otherwise. Under COBRA, the employer may charge the spouse for the full cost of the plan plus a 2% administrative fee.

If you have a question about continued coverage under COBRA, you can call the EMPLOYEE BENEFIT SECURITY ADMINISTRATION toll free at (866) 444-3272 and ask for their latest publication; or visit the HEALTH PLAN AND BENEFITS section of the U.S. Department of Labor Web site for information about COBRA.

 U.S. DEPARTMENT OF LABOR
http://www.dol.gov/

NOT APPLICABLE TO DOMESTIC PARTNER
COBRA being a federal program, does not apply to a Registered Domestic Partner. However, many employers have extended coverage for Domestic Partners. You need to contact the decedent's employer to determine your rights as a Domestic Partner under the decedent's health care plan.

COBRA covers an employer with 20 or more employees. California law regulates group health insurance policies for companies with less than 20 employees. The California Continuation Benefits Replacement Act is called **Cal-COBRA** (Health & Safety 1366.20). The extension period for Cal-COBRA is 36 months — the same as that of COBRA. An important difference is that, under Cal-COBRA, the Spouse/RDP can be charged the full cost of the policy plus an additional 10%. The Spouse/RDP may find it less costly to seek health insurance elsewhere.

If the Spouse/RDP wants to continue with the plan, it is important that he/she notify the health care service plan or the employer just as soon after the death as is practicable. If the employer does not receive notice within 60 days of the date of death, the Spouse/RDP loses the right to continue health care coverage (Health & Safety 1366.24, 1366.25). It is prudent to send notice to both the employer and the health care service plan by registered mail so there is no question about the intent of the spouse/RDP to continue with the plan. For more information about Cal-COBRA visit the Health Insurance section of the California Insurance Web site. http://www.insurance.ca.gov.

SPECIAL COVERAGE FOR SPOUSE/RDP OF DECEASED FIRE FIGHTER OR PEACE OFFICER

The surviving Spouse/RDP and dependent family members of a fire fighter or peace officer who died on or after January 1, 2002, because of an injury or disease arising out of and during the course of his/her official duties are eligible for lifetime health insurance coverage benefits paid for by the state of California (Gov't 22820).

NOTIFY ADVERTISERS

Probably the last person in the world to learn of the decedent's death is the direct mail advertiser. Advertisers are nothing if not tenacious. It is not uncommon for advertisements to be mailed to the decedent for more than ten years after the death. It is not because the advertiser is trying to sell something to the decedent, but rather the people who prepare (and sell) mailing lists do not know that he is dead.

Those who sell mailing lists may not be motivated to update the list because of the cost of doing the necessary research; and perhaps because the price of the mailing list is often based on the number of people on the list. Even those who compose their own list may decide it is less costly to mail to everyone, than take the time (and money) to update the list.

If it gives you pleasure to think of advertisers spending substantial sums for nothing, then that is what you should do (nothing). But for those of you who wince each time you see another piece of mail addressed to the decedent, you can have the Direct Marketing Association place the name of the decedent on their Deceased Do-Not-Contact List. You can do this by registering the decedent's name, address, phone number and E-mail address at the Direct Marketing Association Web site. There is a $1 credit card verification fee. The fee is charged so that the Direct Marketing Association has a record of who registered the decedent's name.

 THE DIRECT MARKETING ASSOCIATION
http://www.the-dma.org

Once registered, members of the Direct Marketing Association are required to remove the decedent's name from their contact list.

If the decedent was someone you named as beneficiary of your insurance policy, Will, Trust, brokerage account or pension plan, you may need to name another in his place:

INSURANCE POLICY ✍

If you named the decedent as the primary beneficiary of your life insurance policy, check to see whether you named a *contingent* (alternate) beneficiary in the event that the decedent did not survive you. If not, you need to contact the insurance company and name a new beneficiary. If you did name a contingent beneficiary, that person is now your primary beneficiary and you need to consider whether you wish to name a new beneficiary at this time.

HEALTH INSURANCE POLICY ✍

If the decedent was covered under your health insurance policy, your employer and the health insurer need to be notified of the death because this may affect the cost of the plan to you and/or your employer.

WILL OR TRUST ✍

Most Wills provide for a contingent beneficiary in the event that the person named as beneficiary dies first. If you named the decedent as your beneficiary, check to see whether you named an alternate beneficiary. If not, you need to have your attorney revise your Will and name a different beneficiary.

Similarly, if you are the Settlor of a Trust and the decedent was one of the beneficiaries of your Trust, check the Trust document to see if you named an alternate beneficiary. If not, contact your attorney to prepare an amendment to the Trust, naming a new beneficiary.

BANK AND SECURITIES ACCOUNTS ✍

If the decedent was a beneficiary or joint owner of your bank or securities account, you may wish to arrange for a new beneficiary or joint owner at this time.

PENSION PLANS ✍

If the decedent was a beneficiary under your pension plan, you need to notify them of the death and name a new beneficiary. Many pension plans require that you notify them within a set period of time (usually 30 days from the date of death), so it is important to notify them as soon as you are able. If the decedent was a beneficiary of your Individual Retirement Account ("IRA") or of your Qualified Retirement Plan ("QRP") and you did not provide for an alternate beneficiary, you need to name another beneficiary.

Before you choose an alternate beneficiary of your pension plan, it is important that you understand all of the options available to you. Not an easy task. There are many complex government regulations relating to IRA and QRP accounts. Even if you believe you understood your options when you set up your account, the federal government often changes those options.

Your choice of beneficiary might impact the amount of money you can withdraw each month, so it is important to consult with your accountant, tax attorney or financial planner, before you make your election.

NOTIFYING CREDITORS

It is the job of the person appointed as Personal Representative to notify the decedent's creditors of the death so that creditors are given an opportunity to come forward and file a *claim* (a written demand for payment) for monies owed. The attorney for the Personal Representative usually takes care of the notice procedure. We will explain that procedure later in this book.

If Probate is not necessary, the next of kin can notify the creditors of the death, but before doing so, it is important to read Chapter 4: WHAT BILLS NEED TO BE PAID? That chapter explains what bills need to be paid and who is responsible to pay them.

Before any bill can be paid, you need to know whether the decedent left any asset that can be used to pay those debts. The next chapter explains how to identify, and then locate, all of the property owned by the decedent.

Locating the Assets 3

It is important to locate the financial records of the decedent and then carefully examine those records. Even the partner in a long-term marriage should conduct a thorough search because the surviving spouse may be unaware of all that was owned (or owed) by the decedent.

It is not unusual for a surviving spouse to be surprised when learning of the decedent's business transactions, especially in those cases where the decedent had control of family finances. One such example is that of Sam and Henrietta. They married just as soon as Sam was discharged from the army. During their marriage, Sam handled all of the finances, giving Henrietta just enough money to run the household.

Every now and again, Henrietta would think of getting a job. She longed to have her own source of income and some economic independence. Each time she brought up the subject Sam would loudly object. He had no patience for this modern wife thing. He got married to have a real wife — one who would cook his meals and keep house for him. He reminded her that the reason they married was because they shared these family values.

Henrietta was not the arguing type. She rationalized, saying that Sam had a delicate stomach and dust allergies. He needed her to prepare his special meals and keep an immaculate house for him. Besides, Sam had a good job with a major cruise line and he needed her to accompany him on his frequent business trips.

Once Sam retired, he was even more cautious in his spending habits. Henrietta seldom complained. She assumed the reason for his "thrift" was that they had little money and had to live on his pension.

They were married 52 years when Sam died at the age of 83. Henrietta was 81 at the time of his death. She was one very happy, very angry and very aged widow when she discovered that Sam left her with assets worth well over a million dollars!

LOCATING RECORDS

As you go through the papers of the decedent, you may come across documents that indicate property ownership, such as bank registers, stock or bond certificates, insurance policies, pension or annuity records, etc. Place all evidence of ownership in a single place. You will need to contact the different companies in order to transfer title to the proper beneficiary.

To obtain the property, you may need to produce evidence of the decedent's personal relationships, such as a marriage or birth certificate, or naturalization papers, or military personnel records. If you cannot locate the decedent's marriage or birth certificate, you can get a copy of those records from the Vital Records office in the state where the event took place. Many states (including California) restrict access to these records to the decedent's Personal Representative or to close family members (Health & Safety 103526). You can use the Internet to locate vital records by using your favorite search engine to find Vital Statistics or Vital Records in the given state.

MILITARY RECORDS

The next of kin can obtain a copy of the military record of a deceased veteran by writing to:

> The National Personnel Records Center
> Military Personnel Records
> 9700 Page Avenue
> St. Louis, MO   63132-5100

They will send you form SF 180 to complete. You can fax your request to them at (314) 801-9195, or you can download the form from the Internet.

 National Archives and Records Administration
http://www.vetrecs.archives.gov

COLLECT AND IDENTIFY KEYS

The decedent may have kept his records in a safe deposit box, so you may find that your first job is to locate the keys to the box. As you go through the personal effects of the decedent, collect and identify all the keys that you find. If you come across an unidentified key, it could be a key to a post office box (private or federal) or a safe deposit box located in a bank or in a private vault company. You will need to determine whether that key opens a box that contains property belonging to the decedent or whether the key is to a box no longer in use. Some ways to investigate are as follows:

☑ CHECK BUSINESS RECORDS

If the decedent kept receipts, look through those items to see if he paid for the rental of a post office or safe deposit box. Also, look at his check register to see if he wrote a check to the Postmaster or to any safe deposit or vault company. Look at his bank statements to see if there is any bank charge for a safe deposit box. Some banks bill separately for safe deposit boxes so check with all of the banks in which the decedent had an account to determine if he had a safe deposit box with that bank.

☑ CHECK THE KEY TYPE

If you cannot identify the key, take it to a local locksmith and ask whether anyone can identify the type of facility that uses such keys. If that doesn't work, go to each bank, post office and private safe deposit box company where the decedent shopped, worked or frequented and ask whether they use the type of key that you found.

☑ CHECK THE MAIL

Check the mail over the next several months to see if the decedent receives a statement requesting payment for the next year's rental of a post office or safe deposit box.

✉ FORWARD THE DECEDENT'S MAIL

You may find evidence of a brokerage account, bank account, or safe deposit box by examining correspondence addressed to the decedent. If he was living alone, have his mail forwarded to the person he named as Personal Representative or Executor of his Will. If the decedent did not leave a Will, and Probate is not necessary, forward the mail to his next of kin. Call the Postmaster and ask him to send you the necessary forms to make the change. Request that the mail be forwarded for the longest period allowed by law (currently one year).

Instead of calling, you can download the change of address form from the U.S. Postal Service Web site.

U.S. POSTAL SERVICE
http://www.usps.com

THE POST OFFICE BOX RENTAL
The decedent may have been renting a post office box at his local post office branch or perhaps at the branch closest to where he did his banking. Ask the Postmaster to help you determine whether the decedent was renting a post office box. If so, you need to locate the key to the box so that you can collect the decedent's mail.

LOST POST OFFICE BOX KEY
If the decedent had a post office box and you cannot locate the key, contact the postmaster and ask him to give you the necessary forms to complete in order to get possession of the mail in that box.

As before, have all mail addressed to that box forwarded to the Personal Representative, or if Probate is not necessary, to the decedent's next of kin.

WHAT TO DO WITH CHECKS

You may receive checks in the mail made out to the decedent. Social Security checks, pension checks and annuity checks issued after the date of death may need to be returned to the sender. See pages 36 and 38 of this book. Other checks need to be deposited. If Probate is necessary, the Personal Representative will open a Probate Estate account and deposit the decedent's checks to that account.

If Probate is not necessary, checks can be deposited to any account held in the name of the decedent. The decedent is not here to endorse the check, but you can deposit it to his account by writing his bank account number on the back of the check and printing beneath it **FOR DEPOSIT ONLY.**

The bank will accept such an endorsement and deposit the check into the decedent's account. The account can then be transferred to the proper beneficiary using an appropriate transfer procedure. Those procedures as described in Chapter 6.

If the check is significant in value or the decedent had different accounts that are accessible to different people, then there needs to be cooperation and a sense of fair play. If not, the dollar gain may not nearly offset the emotional turmoil. That was the case with Gail. Her father made her a joint owner of his checking account to assist in paying his bills. He had macular degeneration and it was increasingly difficult for him to see. The father also had a savings account that was in his name only.

Gail's brother Ken had a good paying job in Alaska. Even though he lived at a distance, Ken, his wife and two children always spent the Christmas holidays with his father and sister. Each summer, their father enjoyed leaving the heat of California to spend a few weeks in the cool Alaskan climate.

One summer, the father purchased a round trip ticket to Alaska. It cost several hundred dollars. Just before the departure date, the father had a heart attack and died. Gail called the airline to cancel the ticket. They refunded the money in a check made out to her father. She deposited the check to the joint account, and then closed it out.

As part of the Probate procedure, the money in the father's savings account was divided equally between Ken and his sister. Ken wondered what happened to the money from the airline tickets.

Gail explained, "Dad paid for the tickets from the joint account, so I deposited the money back to that account. "

"Aren't you going to give me half?"

"Dad meant for me to have whatever was in that joint account. If he wanted you to have half of the money, he would have made you joint owner as well."

Ken didn't see it that way "That refund was part of Dad's Estate. It should have been deposited to his savings account to be divided equally between us. Are you going to force me to argue this in Court?"

Gail finally agreed to split the money with Ken, but the damage was done.

Gail complains that holidays are lonely since Dad died.

LOCATE FINANCIAL RECORDS

To locate the decedent's assets you need to find evidence of what he owned and where those assets are located. As you go through the papers of the decedent you should find documents that indicate property ownership, such as deeds, bank registers, title to motor vehicles, insurance policies, stock or bond certificates, etc. You will need these documents in order to transfer title to the proper beneficiary. Many people keep their financial records in a single place but it is important to check the entire house to be sure you did not miss something.

CHECK THE COMPUTER

Don't overlook that computer sitting silently in the corner. It may hold the decedent's check register and all of his financial records. You may want to monitor his E-mail for E-bank or on-line credit card accounts. The computer may be programmed to protect this information. If you cannot access the decedent's financial records, you may need to employ a computer technician or computer consultant who will be able to print out all of the information on the hard drive of the computer. You can find such a technician or consultant by looking in the telephone book under COMPUTER SUPPORT SERVICES or COMPUTER SYSTEM DESIGNS & CONSULTANTS.

LOCATE OUT OF STATE ACCOUNTS

If the decedent had an out of state bank or securities account, you can locate it through the monthly or quarterly statements mailed to the decedent. Not all companies send out regular statements, but all are required to send out IRS tax form 1099 each year stating the amount of interest or income earned on an account. Once the tax statements come in, you will learn the location of all of the decedent's active and inactive (i.e., closed) accounts.

LOCATE TITLE TO MOTOR VEHICLE

You will need the decedent's certificate of title in order to transfer his car to the proper beneficiary. In California, if monies are owed on a motor vehicle (car, truck, trailer, etc.), the lender takes possession of the original *Certificate of Title* until the loan is paid. If you cannot find the original Certificate, it is either lost or monies are owed on the car and the lienholder has the original title.

You can apply for a duplicate title by downloading Reg 227 (Application for Duplicate Title) from the Department's Web site.

 DEPARTMENT OF MOTOR VEHICLES
http://www.dmv.ca.gov/

You can get a duplicate title by going to the Department of Motor Vehicles ("DMV") in the county of the decedent's residence. You can find the location and telephone numbers of the DMV offices at their Web site.

The DMV will require proof of your authority to get a copy of the Title. In some cases, they will issue the replacement title only to the Personal Representative. It is a good idea to first call the Department at (800) 777-0133 and ask what information they require and the cost of obtaining the replacement Title. For the hearing impaired, the TTY number is (800) 368-4327.

THE ENCUMBERED VEHICLE
You may find that there is a lien on the car for money owed. If so, contact the lienholder and get a copy of the contract that is the basis of the loan. You will need that information before you can transfer title to the beneficiary of the car.

THE LEASED CAR

You may find that the car is leased and not owned by the decedent. If so, contact the lessor and get a copy of the lease agreement. Check to see whether the decedent had life insurance as part of the agreement. If he did, then the lease may now be paid in full and the beneficiary of the car should be able to use the car for the remainder of the leasing period, or take title to the car, whichever option is available under the lease agreement. If the lease is not paid in full upon the decedent's death, arrangements need to be made to satisfy the terms of the agreement. See Chapter 6 for information about transferring a leased car.

 **THE OUT OF STATE CAR**

If the decedent was not a resident of California, he may have a car that is titled and registered in another state. You can get information about titling laws in that state from the AMERICAN ASSOCIATION OF MOTOR VEHICLE ASSOCIATIONS Web site.

 AMERICAN ASSOCIATION OF
MOTOR VEHICLE ASSOCIATIONS
http://www.aamva.org

LOCATE TITLE TO OFF HIGHWAY VEHICLES

An **OFF HIGHWAY VEHICLE** ("OHV") is a motorized vehicle which is operated exclusively off public roads. They include motorcycles, all-terrain vehicles, and snowmobiles. A **SNOWMOBILE** or **OVER SNOW VEHICLE** ("OSV") is a motor vehicle designed to travel over snow on skis, belts, or cleats (Veh. 38012).

Off Highway Vehicles do not require registration in the state of California, however, they must display an identification plate or device issued by the DMV (Veh. 38020). You should find the California Certificate of Title to the OHV. If you cannot locate it, copy the number from the OHV's identification plate, and proceed to obtain a duplicate title from the DMV.

LOCATE TITLE TO WATERCRAFT

The DMV is also in charge of the regulation of watercraft operated within the state. In California, sail-powered vessels over 8' in length and all motor-driven boats must be registered with the DMV. You will find a hull identification number ("HIN") and a vessel registration number (a "CF" number) painted on or permanently attached to the ship (Vehicle 9853, 9853.1, 9853.4).You should also find a pocket sized *Certificate of Number* (Veh. 9853.2).

If you cannot locate the decedent's *Certificate of Ownership*, or Certificate of Number, you can visit your local DMV and obtain duplicate documents by giving them these numbers, or you can write to them at:

Department of Motor Vehicles
ATTN: Vessel Section
P.O. Box 942869
Sacramento, CA 94269-0001

A motor home or *recreational vehicle* that is not permanently attached to real property is considered to be personal property (Health & Safety 18010). It is titled and registered in the same manner as a motor vehicle.

A **manufactured home** and/or a **mobilehome** is a structure built on a permanent chassis (i.e. supporting frame). It is designed for use as a dwelling, with or without a permanent foundation, when connected to the required utilities. It is at least 8 feet wide or 40 feet long and transportable in one or more sections (Health & Safety 18007, 18008).

In order to affix a Mobile/Manufactured home to real property, the owner must obtain a building permit and then a Certificate of Occupancy. Upon receipt of the Certificate of Occupancy, the Department of Motor Vehicles cancels the title and registration to the Mobile/ Manufactured home and has the County Recorder record a document identifying the Registered Owner of the home and the real property where the structure is attached (Health & Safety 18551).

If the decedent owned a mobile/manufactured home that is permanently attached to the land, you should be able to locate the Certificate of Occupancy and the recorded document. If not, contact the County Recorder in the county where the home is located and he will give you a copy of the recorded document. At the same time, check whether there is a record of money owed on the Mobile/ Manufactured Home. If so, you need to contact the lender to determine the terms of the loan agreement.

DETERMINE THE OWNERSHIP OF THE LAND

If the mobile/manufactured home is permanently attached to the land, you need to determine whether the decedent, owned or leased that land. If he owned the land, you should find a deed to the property. See page 79, if you cannot locate the deed to the property.

If the decedent kept his mobile/manufactured home in a leased space, you need to locate the lease to the lot. If you cannot locate the lease, contact the landlord for a copy, and proceed in the same manner as for a residential lease.

 Special Situation DECEDENT'S RESIDENTIAL LEASE

If the decedent was renting his residence, he may have a written lease agreement. It is important to locate the lease because the decedent's Estate may be responsible for payments under the lease. If you cannot find a lease, ask the landlord for a copy. If he reports that there was no written lease, verify that the decedent was on a month to month basis and then work out a mutually agreeable time in which to vacate the premises.

If a written lease is in effect, determine the end of the lease period, and whether the landlord is holding a security deposit. Ask whether he will agree to cancel the lease on condition that the property is promptly vacated and left in good condition. If the landlord wants to hold the Estate responsible to pay the balance of the lease, have your attorney review the lease to determine what rights and responsibilities remain now that the tenant is deceased.

LOCATE TITLE TO AIRCRAFT

If the decedent owned an aircraft, you should find a certificate of title to the aircraft. The Aircraft Registration Branch of the Federal Aviation Administration ("FAA") maintains aircraft records. The Aircraft Registration Branch is located in Oklahoma City, Oklahoma. Aircraft records are open to the general public, but researching the documents yourself may be difficult because the records are maintained by the registration number of the aircraft, and the Aircraft Registration Branch does not furnish lien information or the names of previous owners.

The Aircraft Registration Branch does not perform title searches, however they can give you a list of title search companies. You can call them toll free at (866) 835-5322, or visit their Web site for a list of title companies.

THE FEDERAL AVIATION ADMINISTRATION
http://www.faa.gov

 **LAWYER**

DECEDENT'S ONGOING BUSINESS

If the decedent was the sole owner of a business, or if he owned a partnership interest in a business, the Personal Representative needs to take possession of the decedent's business records and make arrangements for the operation of the business (Probate 9760).

The company accountant or company lawyer may be able to assist in obtaining the records. If you are a beneficiary of the Estate, consider consulting with your own attorney to determine what rights and responsibilities you may have in the business.

COLLECT DEEDS

Collect deeds to all of the *real property* (lot, residential property, condominium) owned by the decedent. In addition to the deed, look for other documents associated with the property, such as a mortgage. You may come across a title insurance policy. The new owner might be able to turn in that policy and receive a discount toward the purchase of a new title insurance, so it is important to keep the policy together with the deed. Instead of a title insurance policy you may find an *Abstract of Title*. An Abstract of Title is a summary of the documents or facts appearing on the public record which affect title to the property. The Abstract will need to be updated once the property is transferred.

THE CONDOMINIUM

The decedent may have owned a condominium. A condominium is a system of individual units. Each owner of the unit has a right to use common areas in the building (Civil 1351(c)). You should find a deed to the unit, and a copy of the *condominium documents* that regulate the complex.

If the decedent owned a condominium and you cannot locate the condominium documents, contact the Condominium Association, or its management company, to get a copy of the documents.

THE STOCK COOPERATIVE

The decedent may have owned a share in a *Stock Cooperative* ("Co-op") The Co-op is usually organized as a corporation with each shareholder of the corporation owning a lease to his own apartment. The Co-op is a legal hybrid in that the share of stock in the Co-op is personal property, however, the lease is *proprietary* because it represents an ownership in real property. In this book, we will consider the Co-op to be real property (Civil 1351 (m)).

If the decedent owned a Co-op, you should find a copy of the stock offering prospectus, stock subscription agreement and the proprietary lease. If you cannot locate these documents, contact the building management and ask them to help you obtain copies of these documents.

CHECK FOR MINERAL RIGHTS

You may find documents associated with rights to real property, such as oil, gas, coal and other mineral rights. These rights may be in the form of royalty interests in the land. If you do not know whether the decedent was receiving royalties, check his last three income tax returns to determine whether he included mineral royalty payments as part of his income.

THE LOST DEED

If you know that the decedent owned real property, but you cannot find the deed, check to see whether he had a safe deposit box. Gaining entry to the box is discussed at the end of this chapter. You can also contact the County Recorder in the county where the property is located. He should be able to provide you with a copy of the last recorded deed.

OUT OF STATE DEEDS

You need to locate the deed to property owned by the decedent in another state or country. You should also look for related documents such as an Abstract of Title, title insurance policy, recorded condominium approval, mortgage etc. If you know the decedent owned out of state real property, but cannot find the deed, you can use the same procedure just described, namely, you can check with the recording department in the county where the property is located. In California, the County Recorder is in charge of the recording department. In other states, it may be the Clerk of the Circuit Court or the Register of Deeds. The clerk in the recording department of the county where the property is located should be able to give you a copy of the last recorded deed.

Many states index the property by the name of the current owner of the property, so if you know the county where the property is located, you should be able to get a copy of the deed by giving the decedent's name to the Clerk. If you do not know the county where the property is located, you will need to wait for the next tax bill. In most states the tax bill contains the name of the current owner and the legal description, or a tax identification number of the property.

The decedent's final federal income tax return needs to be filed. To prepare the return you may need to refer to the returns he filed over the past three years. If you cannot locate his prior tax records, check his personal telephone book and/or his personal bank register to see if he employed someone to prepare his taxes. His tax preparer should have a copy of those records.

If you are unable to locate the decedent's federal tax returns, they can be obtained from the IRS. The IRS will send copies of the decedent's tax filings to anyone who has a *fiduciary relationship* with the decedent. The IRS considers the following people to be a fiduciary:

➤ the person appointed as the Personal Representative of the decedent's Estate

➤ the Successor Trustee of the decedent's Trust

➤ if the person died without a Will, whoever is legally entitled to possession of the decedent's property. See Chapter 5 for an explanation of the Laws of Intestate Succession.

The fiduciary can receive copies of the decedent's tax filings by notifying IRS that he/she is acting in a fiduciary capacity, and then requesting the copies. To notify the IRS of the fiduciary capacity, file Form 56:
NOTICE CONCERNING FIDUCIARY RELATIONSHIP
To request a copy of the tax return, file Form 4506:
REQUEST FOR A COPY OF TAX RETURN

Your accountant can file these forms for you or you can obtain the forms from the IRS by calling (800) 829-3676 or download them from the FORMS section of the IRS Website.

 INTERNAL REVENUE SERVICE
http://www.irs.gov

LOCATE STATE INCOME TAX RETURN

If the decedent earned an income within the state of California, the Personal Representative, or if Probate is not necessary, whoever is entitled to possession of the decedent's property, needs to file a state income tax return (Rev. & Tax 17041, 18566).

You may need last year's return to help prepare the final return. If you cannot locate the decedent's state income tax return you can obtain copies from the California Franchise Tax Board. As with the federal request, you need to be acting in a fiduciary capacity. You will need to complete a Power of Attorney form 3520 and a Request for Tax Return form 3516 and pay a filing fee.

To obtain a copy of these forms, call the Tax Forms Request Unit at (800) 852-5711. If you are calling from out of state, call (916) 845-6600. For the hearing impaired with TDD call (800) 822-6268; or you can write for a copy:

Franchise Tax Board
Tax Forms Request Unit
P.O. Box 307
Rancho Cordova, CA 95741-0307

If the decedent was forgetful, he may have money in a lost bank account or abandoned safe deposit box. Property that is unclaimed is turned over to the California State Comptroller's Office after a period of time as set by California law (Civ. Proc. 1532). The time period depends on the item:

- 3 years from the last transaction on a bank account, including IRA accounts (Civ.Proc. 1513 (a), 1518)
- 3 years from the last safe deposit box transaction (Civ. Proc. 1514)
- 3 years after monies are payable under a life insurance policy or annuity (Civ. Proc. 1515)
- 7 years for an outstanding money order (Civ.Proc 1513 (e).
- 15 years from the date of issue of a travelers check (Civ. Proc. 1513 (c)).

Before turning the property over to the state, the holder of the unclaimed property must make a good faith effort to locate the owner (Civ.Proc. 1513.5). If real property or a tangible item (such as jewelry) remains unclaimed, the Controller will convert it to cash by holding a public auction. Before holding the auction, the Controller will publish notice of the sale in a newspaper of general circulation in the county where the property is located (Civ. Proc. 1373). If the owner (or his heirs) later claims the item, they will receive the net proceeds of the sale.

You can determine whether there is a record identifying the decedent as the owner of abandoned property by calling (800) 992-4647. Out of state, call (916) 323-2827. You can write for information:

DIVISION OF COLLECTIONS
STATE CONTROLLER OFFICE
P.O. Box 942850
Sacramento, CA 94250-5873

You can also get information from the State Controller's Web site.

 CALIFORNIA STATE CONTROLLER'S OFFICE
http://sco.ca.gov/

CLAIMS IN OTHER STATES
Each state has an agency or department that is responsible for handling lost, abandoned or unclaimed property located within that state. If the decedent had residences in other states, call the UNCLAIMED PROPERTY department of the state Comptroller or Treasurer to see if the decedent has unclaimed property in that state. The National Association of Unclaimed Property Administrators lists the Web site of the unclaimed property programs in other states.

 NATIONAL ASSOCIATION OF
UNCLAIMED PROPERTY ADMINISTRATORS
http://www.unclaimed.org

CLAIMS FOR DECEDENT VICTIMS OF HOLOCAUST
The New York State Banking Department has a special Claims Processing Office for Holocaust survivors or their heirs. The office processes claims for Swiss bank accounts that were dormant since the end of World War II. If the decedent was a victim of the Holocaust, you can get information about money that may be due to the decedent's Estate by calling (800) 695-3318.

CLAIMS FOR INCOME TAX REFUNDS

The IRS reports that each year they are unable to deliver thousands of income tax refund checks, mostly because a taxpayer moves and neglects to notify the IRS or the U.S. Postal Service of his new address. In addition to undeliverable income tax refunds, many people are entitled to a refund but no check is sent because they fail to file an income tax return. This is often the case with employees who earned too little income to file a tax return. They may not be aware that taxes withheld from their wages are refundable. Other employees may not have had any tax withheld, but if they had a low income they might be eligible for an Earned Income Tax Credit, provided they file an income tax return. The IRS gives taxpayers three years to claim these funds (26 U.S.C. 6511). There is no penalty for filing a late return in order to qualify for these refunds.

You can determine whether the decedent is entitled to an income tax refund or an Earned Income Tax Credit by calling the IRS at (800) 829-1040. You can also get information about unclaimed tax refunds by visiting the IRS Web site. http://www.irs.gov/

UNCLAIMED STATE TAX REFUNDS
The California Franchise Board also reports that thousands of tax refunds are returned to them each year by the U.S. Postal Service marked "undeliverable." As with the federal income tax return, the decedent may have had a refund due to him that he did not claim. Have an accountant review the decedent's state return for the last three years to determine whether the decedent was entitled to a refund. If you need assistance in obtaining the refund, contact the TAXPAYER ADVOCATE at the Franchise Tax Board at (800) 852-5711.

THE LOST PENSION

The decedent may be entitled to benefits under a pension plan of a prior employer. If the decedent worked for an employer for any significant period of time, say five years or more, check with the company benefit representative to determine whether any pension funds are owed to the decedent. If you are unable to locate the former employer, it could be that the company moved or merged with another company. There are several ways to track down the company, starting with the California Secretary of State, to learn of the company's current status (see page 53). If the company is out of business, or went bankrupt, pension funds may still be available through the PENSION BENEFIT GUARANTY CORPORATION.

CHECK UNCLAIMED PENSION FUNDS

The Pension Benefit Guaranty Corporation is a federal corporation that insures private company pensions. In the year 2007, they reported that there was over $133 million dollars in unclaimed pension benefits. You can call them at (800) 400-7242 to determine whether there is an unclaimed fund for the decedent, or check their Web site.

The Pension Benefit Guaranty Corporation operates an on-line search tool for those employees who did not collect their pension because the company became bankrupt or dissolved the plan, or because the company could not locate the employee. You can search their Web site by decedent's name or by the company name.

PENSION BENEFIT GUARANTY CORPORATION
http://www.pbgc.gov/

HEALTH/COUNTRY CLUB CONTRACT

If the decedent belonged to a gym, health club, or country club, he may have prepaid for the year. Look for the club contract. It will give the terms of the agreement. If you cannot locate the contract, contact the company for a copy of the agreement. If the contract was prepaid, determine whether the agreement provides for a refund for the unused portion.

Even if the contract does not provide for a refund, you may be able to get the owner of the club to agree to assigning the remaining membership to an heir of the decedent's Estate. Such an assignment is good public relations as well as a means of generating new business should the heir decide to purchase his own membership.

SERVICE CONTRACT

Many people purchase appliance service contracts to have their appliances serviced in the event that an appliance should need repair. If the decedent had a security system then he may have had a service contract with a company to monitor the system and contact the police in the event of a break-in.

If the decedent had a service contract, then you need to locate it and determine whether it can be assigned to the new owner of the property. If the contract is assignable, the new owner can reimburse the decedent's Estate for the unused portion. If the contract cannot be assigned, then once the property is transferred, try to obtain a refund for the unused portion of the contract.

FILING THE WILL WITH THE COURT

Anyone who has possession of the decedent's original Will needs to file it with Court within 30 days of being notified of the death (Probate 8200 (a)). If the decedent was a resident of the state of California, the Will needs to be deposited with the Clerk of the Superior Court in the county of the decedent's residence (Probate 7051). You can find directions to the court house on the Internet at the Web site of the National Center For State Courts.

 NATIONAL CENTER FOR STATE COURTS
http://www.ncsconline.org

The Court will accept an original Will only and not a copy, so it is important to hand carry the original document to the Court. If you are the Executor or Personal Representative named in the Will, you can give it to your attorney to file when he begins the Probate procedure. Make a copy of the Will for your own records before delivering it to the Court or to your attorney, but don't alter the Will by removing its staples.

If the Will is in your possession and you are not the named Executor or Personal Representative, you need to deliver the Will to the Clerk of the Superior Court of the county where the Estate is to be administered and mail a copy of the Will to the person named as Executor (or Personal Representative). If you do not know his where abouts, you can mail a copy to anyone named as a beneficiary of the Will (Probate 8200).

If the decedent owned property in California, but did not live here, the Will can be deposited with the Clerk in the county where the decedent's property is located (Probate 7052). However, read the next page before doing so.

 **LAWYER**

PROBATING THE OUT OF STATE PROPERTY

If the decedent had his residence in California and owned property in another state, you may need to conduct the initial Probate in California and an *ancillary* (secondary) Probate in the other state. If the decedent had his residence in another state and owned property in California, it may need to be the other way around. You may need to conduct the initial Probate in the other state (Probate 12510).

If you are going to be Personal Representative, and the decedent was a resident of another state, before depositing the Will with the Court, consult with an experienced Probate attorney in each state to determine where the initial Probate should be conducted. Convenience is important, but there are other things to consider:

COST OF PROBATE Ask each attorney whether the location of the initial Probate procedure will have an effect on the total cost of Probate.

WHO INHERITS THE INTESTATE ESTATE Intestate laws vary significantly state to state. In particular, most states have no provision for a surviving Domestic Partner. If the decedent died without a Will, it is important to determine whether the location of the initial Probate will change the amount each heir will inherit.

ESTATE/INHERITANCE TAXES
Determine whether the location of the initial procedure will have an impact on the amount of taxes that need to be paid.

WILL DRAFTED IN ANOTHER STATE OR COUNTRY

A Will that was drafted in another state or country can be accepted into Probate in California, provided:

☑ the Will was prepared and signed according to the laws of the state where it was signed

- or -

☑ if the decedent was a resident of another state, the Will was prepared and signed according to the laws of that state

- or -

☑ the Will was prepared and signed according to California law (Probate 8002).

See Chapter 5 for a discussion of what constitutes a valid Will in California.

WILL DRAFTED IN ANOTHER LANGUAGE

A Will that is written in a foreign language must be accompanied by a true and complete English translation before it can be admitted to Probate (Probate 8002(b)2). If the Will is in a language other than English, consult with an attorney to determine what proof the judge will require in order to accept the translated Will into Probate as a true and correct translation of the original.

THE MISSING WILL

People tend to put off making a Will until they think they need to. For many, that need arises when they are elderly and/or seriously ill and have property that they want to leave to someone. It is uncommon for a young person to have a Will; but those who are elderly, with significant assets, usually have one. A survey conducted for the American Association of Retired Persons ("AARP") found that the probability of having a Will increases with age. Forty-four percent of those surveyed who were between the ages of 50 and 54 had a Will. This increased to 85% for those 80 and older.

Those who make a Will usually tell the person they appoint as Executor of the existence of the Will. Chances are, someone in the decedent's circle of family and friends, knows whether there is a Will. If you believe that the decedent had a Will, but you cannot find it, there are at least three places to check out:

⇨   **THE DECEDENT'S ATTORNEY**

Look at the decedent's checkbook for the past few years and see whether he paid any attorney fees. If you are able to locate the decedent's attorney, call and inquire whether he ever drafted a Will for the decedent, and if so, whether he has the original Will in his possession. If he does, he will, within 30 days, deliver the Will to the Clerk of the Superior Court of the county where Probate can take place. California law requires that he also mail a copy of the Will to the person named as Executor or Personal Representative of the Will, and that he do these things without charge (Probate 8200).

Having the decedent's attorney to forward the Will to the Court does not obligate you to employ him should you later find that you need the assistance of an attorney for the Probate administration

⇨ **THE CLERK OF THE PROBATE COURT**

As explained, California law requires that whoever has the original Will must deposit it with the Probate Court within 30 days of being notified of the death (Probate 8200 (a)). It is a good idea to check with the Clerk in the county where the decedent lived in the chance that someone found the Will and filed it with the Court.

⇨ **THE SAFE DEPOSIT BOX**

Some people keep their original Will in a safe deposit box. If you believe that the decedent had a Will but you cannot find it, then check to see if the decedent had a safe deposit box. If he did, you will need to gain entry to that box to see whether the Will is in the box. See page 93 for an explanation of how to gain entry to the safe deposit box.

 **LAWYER**

A COPY OF THE WILL AND NO ORIGINAL

A person can revoke his Will simply by destroying it i.e., by ripping it up, or by writing over it in such a way as to indicate that the Will is cancelled or revoked (Probate 6120). If you have a copy of the Will and cannot find the original, the Probate judge will presume that the decedent revoked his Will by destroying it.

If you believe the original was not revoked but is lost, you can ask the Probate Court to admit a copy of the Will to Probate (Probate 8223). But in general, if a Will cannot be found and it was last seen in the possession of the decedent, the Court will presume that the decedent revoked it.

Courts have allowed a missing Will to be entered into Probate, provided it can be proven that it was in the existence as of the date of death, or it was destroyed during the Will maker's lifetime, fraudulently, or because of some calamity, and without his knowledge (*Estate of Bristol*, 23 Cal.2d 221 (1943)).

Not easy things to prove. If you wish to have a lost Will admitted to Probate, you will need to employ an attorney experienced in Probate matters to present your case to the Court.

ACCESSING THE SAFE DEPOSIT BOX

If the decedent rented a safe deposit box with another person, each with free access to the box, the surviving joint renter is free to go to the box and remove its contents. But if the safe deposit box was in the decedent's name only, access to the box is limited. If you have the key to the box you may enter the box for the limited purpose of removing the Will, any Trust document, and any instruction for the disposition of the decedent's remains. If the key to the safe deposit box cannot be found, it will take permission from the Court, or the appointment of a Personal Representative, in order to inspect the contents of the box.

The bank will allow access only under the supervision of one of its officers or employees. Before going to the bank, call and make an appointment to meet with an officer of the company. You will need to give the bank proof of your identity and proof of the decedent's death. Most banks will want to see a certified copy of the death certificate. The law allows a written statement from the Coroner or the treating physician as proof of death (Probate 331(b)(1). If you do not want to wait until you receive the death certificate, ask the bank whether such written statement will be acceptable to them.

GETTING THE CONTENTS OF THE SAFE DEPOSIT BOX
If the Will or Trust is found in the box, the person gaining access to the box may remove these items after the officer or employee makes a copy of the documents (Probate 331(d)(3)). The bank has the right to charge a reasonable fee to copy these documents.

Before leaving the bank, ask an officer to give you a copy of the inventory of the contents of the box using the company letterhead. You may need the inventory to present to the Court to get an order giving you authority to take possession of the contents of the safe deposit box. If you find the original Will in the safe deposit box, you need to deliver the Will to the Clerk of the Superior Court in the county of the decedent's residence. If the decedent did not live in California, you can deposit the Will in the county where safe deposit box is located. As explained earlier, in addition to depositing the Will with the Court, you are required to mail or deliver a copy of the Will to the named Executor (Probate 8200).

If you find other valuables in the box, you might need to go through a Probate procedure to get possession of those items. See Chapter 6 for an explanation of what type of Probate procedure may be necessary in order to get possession of the contents of the safe deposit box.

After examining the contents of the box, determine whether it is necessary to keep the box open during the administration of the Estate, or whether the lease can be cancelled and monies refunded to the decedent's Estate.

Once you have located the decedent's property you may think the next step is to determine who gets to inherit that property. But some of that property may be needed to pay monies owed by the decedent; so the next step is to determine what, if any, bills need to be paid.

And that is the topic of the next chapter.

What Bills Need To Be Paid? 4

The Personal Representative has the duty to be sure that all valid *claims* (demands for payment) are paid. If the decedent had debts, but no money or property, then of course there is no way to pay a claim against the decedent's Estate. The only remaining question is whether anyone else is responsible to pay for the monies owed. If the decedent was married, the first person the creditor will look to is the decedent's spouse. To understand the basis of this expectation, you need to know a bit of the history of our legal system.

Our laws are derived from the English Common Law. Under early English Common Law, a single woman had the right to own property in her own name and also the right to contract to buy or sell property; but when she married, her legal identity merged with her spouse. She could not hold property free from her husband's claim or control. She could no longer enter into a contract without her husband's permission.

Once married, a woman became financially dependent on her husband. He, in turn, became legally responsible to provide his wife with basic necessities — food, clothing, shelter and medical services. If anyone provided basic necessities to his wife, then regardless of whether the husband agreed to be responsible for the debt, he became obliged to pay for them. This law was called the DOCTRINE OF NECESSARIES.

States in America departed from English Common Law by enacting a series of Married Women's Rights Acts. The California legislature passed a Married Woman's Rights law giving a married woman the right to own property, and the right to enter into a contract (Family 721).

Court cases followed that tested whether the Doctrine of Necessaries still applied. Judges had to decide:

If a wife can own property and contract to pay for her own necessities, should her husband be responsible for such debts in the event she does not have enough money to pay for them?

And if the husband is responsible for his wife's necessities, should she be responsible for his?

In California, the answer to both of these questions is "yes." Although some states abolished the law altogether, other states, including California, decided to apply the Doctrine equally to both sexes, making the husband responsible to pay for his wife's necessities and the wife responsible to pay for her husband's necessities (Family 914).

As explained earlier, a Registered Domestic Partner has all of the rights and responsibilities of a married partner (Family 297.5). This being the case, a Registered Domestic Partner is responsible to pay for the necessities of his partner, regardless of whether (s)he agreed to do so.

COMMUNITY PROPERTY LIABILITY

California is a Community Property state, so in addition to making the Spouse/RDP liable to pay for necessities, the Spouse/RDP could be responsible to pay for the other's debts provided there is **Community Property** available. Community Property is property acquired by either Domestic Partner while living in California or by a husband or wife while they are married and living in California (Family 760). This does not include items either party inherits or receives as a gift during the marriage.

If a married couple lived in another state during the course of their marriage, property they acquired as a married couple in another state is called **Quasi-community property** (Family 125). The laws relating to Quasi-community property are much the same as those for Community Property. For simplicity, we will use the term "Community Property" understanding that the law quoted applies to Quasi-community property as well.

Separate Property is anything owned by a Spouse/RDP prior to their union and property acquired by a Spouse/RDP during their union as a gift or an inheritance. Any profit or increase in value of Separate Property is also Separate Property (Family 770). For example, if a husband owned rental property prior to his marriage, any money he receives as rent is Separate Property. If the property appreciates in value, that increase in value is also Separate Property. If the couple separate, money earned while they are separated, is also Separate Property (Family 771).

COMMUNITY PROPERTY OWNERSHIP IS OPTIONAL

Couples can enter into a *Premarital Agreement* or *Pre-partnership Agreement* prior to their union stating what property will be Separate Property and what property will be their Community Property. If they wish, they can agree that all of their property is to be owned as Separate Property, i.e., they will not own any Community Property. In the absence of a Pre-partnership Agreement, property owned by the couple is considered to be Community Property. However, at any time during the union, the couple can sign an Agreement identifying certain of their property as being owned separately. Any transfer of Community Property to Separate Property, or Separate to Community, needs to be in writing (Family 852).

COMMUNITY DEBT VS. SEPARATE DEBT

A *Community Debt* is a debt which both parties agreed to pay, or a debt incurred for the benefit of the family. All of the couple's property (Community or Separate) is available to pay for a Community Debt. If the non-contracting Spouse/RDP is required to use his/her Separate Property to pay for the necessities of the other and the debtor has Community Property or Separate Property, the non-contracting partner is entitled to be reimbursed from those funds — unless the non-contracting Spouse/RDP was obliged to pay for the necessities by Court order, or by the written Agreement of the parties (Family 914 (b)).

A *Separate Debt* is a money owed by one party prior to the marriage, or a liability incurred by one partner only, that is not for the benefit of the family. The debtor must use his Separate Property to pay for his Separate Debt. However, if that is not enough, all of the couple's Community Property is available to pay for the debt (Civ. Proc. 695.020).

In general, the Separate Property of the non-debtor Spouse/RDP is not available to pay for the Separate Debt of the debtor Spouse/RDP (Family 1000).

LIABILITY AFTER DEATH

The rules governing what monies are available to pay the debts of a deceased Spouse/RDP are complex and beyond the scope of this book. But, in general, all of the couple's Community Property is available to pay a Community Debt (Probate 11444).

If the decedent left a Separate Debt, it needs to be paid from his Separate Property. Under California law, the decedent's funeral expenses and the expenses of his last illness are considered to be his Separate Debt (Probate 11446). If there is not enough Separate Property to pay for the decedent's Separate Debt, his share of their Community Property is available to pay the debt.

That share is available even of the surviving Spouse/RDP now owns the property without any need for Probate. For example, suppose the couple acquired an expensive painting during their union. That painting now belongs to the surviving Spouse/RDP, but the decedent's creditor can demand that the surviving Spouse/RDP use the decedent's half of the value of the painting to satisfy that debt (Probate 13550, 13551).

Of course, if the couple signed an Agreement stating that the painting is not Community Property, or if the painting was received as a gift, or an inheritance by the surviving spouse/RDP, it is Separate Property and is not accessible to the decedent's creditors (Family 770).

JOINT DEBTS

A *joint debt* is a debt that two or more people are responsible to pay. Usually the contract or promissory note states that the parties agree to *joint and several liability*, meaning they all agree to pay the debt and each of them promises to be personally responsible to pay the debt. A joint debt can also be in the form of monies owed by one person with payment guaranteed by another person. If the person who owes the money does not pay, the *guarantor* (the person who guaranteed payment) is responsible to make payment.

SPOUSE	JOINT SPOUSAL DEBTS

Loans signed by the decedent and his Spouse/RDP are joint debts, as are charges on credit cards that both were authorized to use. Property taxes are a joint debt if the decedent and the spouse both owned the property. All of these debts may be paid from the decedent's Estate. If there are insufficient Estate funds, the surviving spouse is liable for the entire debt.

As explained earlier, even if the surviving Spouse/RDP did not agree to be responsible for the debt, (s)he may be responsible to pay money owed by the decedent, depending on whether Community Property is available.

JOINT PROPERTY BUT NO JOINT DEBT

Suppose all of the decedent's funds are owned jointly with a family member (not his Spouse/RDP) and the joint owner of the bank account did not agree to pay those debts? Can the decedent's creditor require that half of the joint funds be set aside to pay the debt?

The answer depends on how the account was set up. When a bank account is established the owners of the account sign an agreement with the bank stating who is to receive the funds should one of the joint owners die. If the account was set up as *Tenants In Common*, there are is no right of survivorship. The decedent's *net contribution* (what he contributed to the account less what he withdrew) becomes part of his Estate and is available to pay his debts. That is not the case if the account was owned as *Joint Tenants with Right of Survivorship*. California courts have ruled that the surviving owner of a Joint Account With Right of Survivorship owns all of the account as of the date of death. The decedent's creditors cannot require payment from that account (*Ziegler v. Bonnell*, 126 P.2d 118, (Cal.1942)).

NO EXEMPTION FOR TAXES

The surviving owner of the decedent's joint survivorship account has no obligation to use the joint account funds to pay the decedent's creditors; however, the decedent's share of the account is included as part of the decedent's **Taxable Estate**. If federal or state taxes are due, whoever takes the decedent's share of the joint account may be required to pay whatever taxes are due on the decedent's share of the account.

NO MONEY — NO PROPERTY

If the decedent owed money, the debt needs to be paid from assets owned by the decedent — which leads to the next question, "Did the decedent have any money in his own name when he died?"

If the decedent died without any money or property in his name, then there is no money to pay any creditor. The only question that remains is whether anyone else is liable to pay those bills. The issue of payment most often arises in relation to services provided by nursing homes. When a person enters a nursing home, he is usually too ill to speak for himself or even sign his name. In such cases, the nursing home administrator may ask the spouse or a family member to sign a battery of papers on behalf of the patient before allowing the patient to enter the facility. Buried in that battery of papers may be a statement that the family member agrees to be responsible for payment to the nursing home. If the family member refuses to guarantee payment and the patient's finances are limited, the facility may refuse to admit the patient.

Under the Federal Nursing Home Reform Law, a nursing home that accepts Medicare or Medicaid payments is prohibited from requiring a family member to guarantee payment as a condition of allowing the patient to enter that facility (42 U.S.C. 13951-3(c)(5)(A)(ii)).

This is not a problem if the patient is married, because the patients spouse is responsible to pay for his necessities. However, if the patient is single, this presents a dilemma for the nursing home. They cannot require the family member to guarantee payment, but if the patient runs out of money no one is responsible to make payments should the patient's monies run out.

Most nursing homes are business establishments and not charitable organizations. Even not-for-profit organizations must cover their costs. The nursing home must be paid for the services they provide or they soon will be out of business. For an insolvent patient, the solution is to have the patient admitted to the facility as a Medicaid patient.

But suppose the decedent had some money when he entered the nursing home and you agreed to guarantee payment to the nursing home. Did you feel that you were coerced into signing as a guarantor?

If your family member died without funds, are you now responsible to pay the decedent's final nursing home bill?

An experienced Elder Law attorney will be able to answer these questions after examining the documents you signed and the conditions under which the patient entered the nursing home.

PAYING THE DECEDENT'S BILLS

If the decedent was married and Probate is not necessary, the surviving spouse needs to make arrangements to pay their joint debts. If the decedent was not married and he owned property belonging to him alone, such as a bank account, securities or real property, the job of paying money owed by the decedent falls to the Personal Representative.

As soon as he is appointed, the Personal Representative is required to make a diligent effort to locate all of the decedent's creditors and notify them that they have a right to file a claim against the decedent's Estate for money owed (Probate 9050).

The Personal Representative needs to look over each claim and decide whether that claim is valid. The problem with making that decision is that the decedent is not here to say whether he actually received the goods and services that are now being billed to his Estate.

That is especially the case for medical or nursing care bills. An example of improper billing brought to the attention of this author was that of a bill submitted for a physical examination of the decedent. The bill listed the date of the examination as July 10th, but the decedent died on July 9th. Other incorrect billings may not be as obvious, so each invoice needs to be carefully examined.

If the Personal Representative decides to challenge a bill, and is unable to settle the matter with the creditor, the Probate Court will decide whether the debt is valid and needs to be paid.

MEDICAL BILLS COVERED BY INSURANCE

If the decedent had health insurance you may receive an invoice stamped "THIS IS NOT A BILL." This means the health care provider has submitted the bill to the decedent's health insurance company and expects to be paid by them. If the decedent was receiving Medicare, you will receive a *Medicare Summary Notice* listing all of the services or supplies that were billed to Medicare for the prior 30 days. If the decedent was receiving Medicare Part B drugs, such as certain cancer drugs, you may receive two Medicare Summary Notices, one for the doctor's visit and one for medication given to the decedent during the visit. The medication notice will state whether the doctor administered drug was approved or denied.

Even though payment is not requested, it is important to verify that the bill is valid for two reasons:

➤ LATER LIABILITY

If the insurer refuses to pay the claim, the facility will seek payment from whoever is in possession of the decedent's property, and that may reduce the amount inherited by the beneficiaries.

➤ INCREASED HEALTH CARE COSTS

Regardless of whether the decedent was covered by a private health care insurer or Medicare, improper billing increases the cost of health insurance to all of us. Consumers pay high premiums for health coverage. We, as taxpayers, all share the cost of Medicare. If unnecessary or fraudulent billing is not checked, then ultimately, we all pay. If you believe that you have come across a case of Medicare fraud, you can call the ANTI-FRAUD HOTLINE (800) 447-8477 and report the incident to the Office of the Inspector General of the United States Department of Health and Human Services.

HOW TO CHECK MEDICARE BILLING

The structure of Medicare has changed giving people the option of staying with the *Original Medicare Plan* or choosing a *Medicare Advantage Plan* such as a Medicare Health Maintenance Organization ("HMO"), or other Medicare Health Plans. Coverage depends on which plan is chosen. You need to determine whether the decedent was covered under the Original Medicare Plan, or some other Medicare Plan. The publication *Medicare and You* explains coverage under the different options. See page 55 of this book, to obtain a copy of the booklet. Coverage under any of the other plans is explained in the membership materials given to the decedent at the time he signed up for the plan.

BILLING UNDER THE ORIGINAL MEDICARE PLAN

ASSIGNMENT

An important billing question for those under the Original Medicare Plan is whether the health care provider agreed to accept Medicare *assignment*, meaning that they agreed to accept the Medicare-approved amount. If so, the patient is responsible to pay any Medicare deductible and coinsurance amounts (usually 20% of the approved amount).

Doctors and health care providers who do not accept assignment, are limited in the amount they can charge for a Medicare covered service. The highest they can charge is **15%** over the Medicare-approved amount. This *Limiting Charge* applies only to certain services and does not apply to supplies and equipment. For more information about assignment you can call (800) 633-4227 for your free copy of *Does your doctor or supplier accept "assignment?"* or you can down-load the publication from the Medicare Website.
http://www.medicare.gov

ADVANCE BENEFICIARY NOTICE

For those who are in the Original Medicare Plan, a doctor or a supplier may give notice saying that Medicare probably will not pay for the service that is about to be provided. This is called an *Advance Beneficiary Notice*.

Other Medicare Plans also notify the patient in the event that the service is not covered under the plan. If the patient still wants the service after receiving such notice, he will be asked to sign an agreement stating that he will pay for the service in the event that Medicare does not pay.

If all of this appears confusing, it is.
To check the decedent's Medicare billing, you need the answers to the following questions:

What is the plan?

Determine whether the decedent was in the Original Medicare Plan or some other Medicare Health Plan.

What is covered under the plan?

The *Medicare and You* booklet explains what is covered under the Original Medicare Plan. You will need a copy of the membership materials for the Medicare Advantage Plans to determine what is covered under that plan.

Does the Provider accept Assignment?

If the decedent was in the Original Medicare Plan, you need to determine whether the health care provider accepted assignment; and if not, whether the Limiting Charge applies to the services provided. If assignment is accepted, or the Limiting Charge applies, you need to determine the Medicare-approved amount.

Did the decedent agree to pay?

Check to see whether the decedent was given notice that the service would not be covered by Medicare; and if so, whether he signed a contract agreeing to pay in the event that Medicare refuses to pay.

Did the decedent have a Medigap Policy?

A **Medigap Policy** is a health insurance policy sold by private insurance companies in accordance with state and federal law. It is Medicare Supplemental Insurance. If the decedent had a Medigap Policy, get a copy of the contract and see if the goods or services provided are covered under the Policy.

DENIAL OF MEDICARE COVERAGE

If the health care provider reports to you that a service provided to the decedent is not covered by Medicare, or if the facility submits the bill and Medicare refuses to pay, check to see if you agree with that ruling by getting answers to the questions on the prior page. You can appeal that decision if you believe that the decedent was wrongly denied coverage.

If the decedent was in the Original Medicare Plan, you will find information about how to file an appeal on the Medicare Summary Notice. If he opted for a Medicare Advantage Plan or some other Medicare Health Plan, you will find that information in his health care plan materials. The book *Your Medicare Rights and Protections* (CMS Pub. No. 10112) contains information about appeals. You can get a free copy by calling (800) 633-4227 or by down-loading it from the Medicare Website. http://www.medicare.gov.

The U.S. Department of Health and Human Services is in charge of Medicare Appeals. They hold hearings with video conference equipment or by telephone. They allow you to appeal in person before an Administrative Law Judge only if "special or extraordinary circumstances exist."

Even if an in-person hearing is allowed, a hearing before an Administrative Law Judge is currently available (for the year 2007) at only four locations — Miami, Florida; Cleveland, Ohio; Irvine, California and Arlington, Virginia. Those who insist on a face-to-face hearing lose their right to receive a decision within 90 days, so it may take considerable time before the matter is settled.

GETTING HELP WITH THE APPEAL

You can appeal the decision yourself, but it is best to first call the State Health Insurance Program ("SHIP") and learn how to proceed with your appeal. In California, the **HEALTH INSURANCE COUNSELING AND ADVOCACY PROGRAM** administers the SHIP program. You can call them at (800) 434-0222.

If you want an attorney to assist with your appeal, call the California Bar at (866) 442-2529for a referral to an attorney experienced in Medicare appeals. Out of state call (415) 538-2250. Some attorneys work *pro bono* (literally for the public good; i.e. without charge) but most charge to assist in an appeal. Federal statute 42 U.S.C. 406(a)(2)(A) limits the amount an attorney may charge for a successful Medicare appeal to 25% of the amount recovered or $4,000, whichever is the smaller amount.

Medicaid is a federal and state program that provides medical and long term nursing care for people with low income and limited resources. In California, it is called **Medi-Cal**. Federal law requires the state to recover monies spent from the Estate of a Medi-Cal recipient who was 55 or older when the decedent received Medi-Cal assistance for nursing home care or for home based care or for other community based services (42 U.S.C. 1396(p)).

There usually is no money to recover because to qualify for Medicaid in California, a person may not have more than $2,000 in assets. But sometimes it happens that the Medicaid recipient dies and his Estate receives money perhaps as part of a settlement of a lawsuit. Also, it could happen that he owned a home that was in his name only.

Owning a home will not disqualify a person from receiving Medi-Cal, provided the equity in the home does not exceed $500,000. But once the Medi-Cal recipient dies, the state has the right to place a lien on that home and seek recovery from the proceeds of the sale of the house once he dies.

Federal and state law prohibits the foreclosure of that lien until the surviving spouse, and/or the decedent's minor or disabled child are no longer living in the home (42 U.S.C. 1396(p)), Welf. & Inst. 14009.5).

The state has the right to foreclose the lien against the homestead once the surviving spouse dies. This being the case, the Director Of Health Services must be notified, not only when the Medi-Cal recipient dies, but when his surviving spouse dies as well. It is the job of the Estate attorney to give such notice within 90 days of the death. If there is no attorney, the Personal Representative needs to notify the Director of the death. If Probate is not necessary, whoever takes possession of the decedent's Estate needs to send the Director a copy of the death certificate (Probate 215).

If you have a question about claims against the decedent's Estate you can call (800) 541-5555 or you can visit the Department of Health Services.

 DEPARTMENT OF HEALTH SERVICES — MEDI-CAL
http://www.medi-cal.ca.gov

Sometimes it happens that the decedent had money or property titled in his name only, but he also had a significant amount of debt. In such cases the beneficiaries may wonder whether they should go through a Probate procedure if there will be little, if anything, left after the creditors are paid. Before making the decision consider that some assets are protected under California law:

✧ PENSION PLANS ✧

Annuities, pensions, profit sharing or other retirement plans regulated by the federal Employee Retirement Income Security Act of 1974 ("ERISA"), including IRA accounts and plans identified by the Internal Revenue Code as 408, 408A, are creditor proof (Civ. Proc. 704.115). Monies received by a beneficiary of such plans are protected from the decedent's creditors with the following exceptions:

NO EXEMPTION FOR SPOUSAL OR CHILD SUPPORT

The decedent's pension is not exempt from money he owed for spouse or child support (Civ. Proc. 704.115 (c)).

NO EXEMPTION FOR TAXES

In general, income taxes are not paid when money is placed in a retirement plan. Taxes are paid when the monies are withdrawn from the account regardless of whether the monies are withdrawn by the retiree or the person he named as beneficiary of the retirement plan. If you inherit money from the decedent's pension, retirement allowance, or annuity, you may need to pay taxes on these monies. You should consult with an accountant or an attorney to determine how much money to set aside to pay for federal and state income taxes (Civ. Proc. 704.115 (a)(3)).

✧ LIFE INSURANCE PROCEEDS

Life insurance proceeds paid to the surviving Spouse/RDP, or a dependent, as a result of the decedent's death are exempt from the claims of the decedent's creditors but only to the extent that the proceeds are necessary for the support of the Spouse/RDP and/or dependents of the decedent. (Civ. Proc. 704.100 (c)).

If the policy is in the form of a single payment, how much of that policy is necessary for their support may be challenged by a creditor. If the life insurance policy is in the form of an endowment or annuity policy with monthly payments to the spouse or dependent, it may be easier to establish that the money is needed for their support.

✧ WRONGFUL DEATH AWARD

As discussed in Chapter 1, the family has the right to bring a law suit if the decedent died because of the wrongful act of another. The amount awarded to the surviving Spouse/RDP or to a dependent relative is exempt from the claims of their creditors to the extent reasonably necessary for their support (Civ. Proc. 704.150).

✧ THE HOMESTEAD EXEMPTION ✧

California homeowners are entitled to creditor protection for their **homestead**, i.e., their principal residence. The amount of protection varies with the circumstances. The amount of creditor protection depends on the status of the decedent when he died:

➪ $75,000 if the decedent was living with a Spouse/RDP or a family member who is not an owner of the residence.

➪ $150,000 if the decedent or his Spouse/RDP was 65 or older.

➪ $150,000 if the decedent was disabled and unable to work. If he was receiving social security disability benefits he probably qualified for this exemption.

➪ $150,000 if the decedent was 55 or older with a gross annual income of $15,000 or less — or his combined gross annual income with his Spouse/RDP is $20,000 or less.

➪ $50,000 for everyone else (Civ. Proc. 704.730).

If the decedent owned money and a creditor had a judgment lien on the home, the creditor protection continues for the benefit of the Spouse/RDP or a family member living in the home (Civ. Proc. 704.995). For example, suppose the decedent was a disabled, 70 year old homeowner who was living with his daughter. If he left the property to his daughter, his $150,000 Homestead Creditor Exemption continues after his death. If there was a judgment lien on his home for $100,000, and his homestead is appraised at $200,000 at the time of his death, his creditor can force the sale of the property to pay the debt. The daughter will inherit the first $150,000 of the proceeds of the sale. The remaining $50,000 will go to the judgment creditor.

✧ EXEMPT PROPERTY ✧

In addition to the Homestead Exemption, the surviving Spouse/RDP and/or minor child of the decedent can ask the Court to allow them to keep any of his property that was exempt from the enforcement of a money judgment against the decedent (Probate 6510, 6520). This includes:

⇨ Up to $1,150 in jewelry

⇨ Household furnishings, appliances, books, musical instruments, etc. provided any particular item is not greater than $450 in value

⇨ Up to $2,775 of value in one motor vehicle

⇨ Up to $17,425 of monies awarded to the decedent because of personal bodily injury

⇨ Any award granted to the decedent under the Crime Victim's Reparation Law

⇨ Up to $1,750 of value in the professional books, or tools of the trade.

NOTE The above figures are those in effect as we went to print in 2007. See statute Civil Procedure 703.140 for a complete list of *Exempt Property* and their current values.

SMALL ESTATE SET-ASIDE

If the decedent left a Spouse/RDP and minor children, and the value of his Estate, not counting the Homestead, is not greater than $20,000, instead of taking the above Exempt property, the Spouse/RDP can ask the Court to assign all of the decedent's Estate to the Spouse/RDP and/or the minor children. The only problem with asking for an assignment is that the Court will still require funeral expenses, costs of last illness and the expenses of Probate be paid and the property to be assigned subject to all pending liens, i.e., the Spouse/RDP is responsible to pay money owed on the property (Probate 6609).

✧ THERE IS A PRIORITY OF PAYMENT ✧

The next thing to consider is that not all debts are equal. California statute (Probate 11420) establishes an order of priority for payment of claims made against the decedent's Estate:

CLASS 1: COST OF ADMINISTRATION

Top priority goes to the cost of the Probate proceeding including attorney's fees and fees charged by the Personal Representative.

CLASS 2: SECURED DEBTS

If the decedent has a *secured debt* such as a mortgage on a house, or a car loan, or even a judgment lien on property owned by the decedent, then those debts have priority to the extent of the value of the secured item. For example, suppose the decedent owed $10,000 on a car, but the car is worth only $8,000, the creditor can take possession of the car. The remaining $2,000 becomes a general debt against the Estate (see Class 7).

CLASS 3: FUNERAL EXPENSES

Third in priority are the decedent's funeral expenses.

CLASS 4: EXPENSES OF LAST ILLNESS

All of the decedent's medical and nursing expenses associated with his last illness are fourth in priority.

CLASS 5: FAMILY ALLOWANCE

If the decedent was supporting a spouse/DP, child or parent, then they are entitled to receive money for their maintenance during the Probate. The amount of the **Family Allowance** is set by the Court. If there is not enough money to pay all of the decedent's creditors, the Family Allowance must end no later than one year after the Court issues Letters to the Personal Representative (Probate 6540, 6543).

CLASS 6: WAGE CLAIMS

If within 90 days of his death, the decedent employed someone and the employee is owed wages, that claim is 6th in priority of payment. Claims in this class are limited to $2,000 per employee. Anything over $2,000 becomes a Class 7 debt.

CLASS 7: ALL OTHER DEBTS

No payment can be made to a given class until monies owed to those in a prior class are paid. And there are no priorities within a given class. For example, suppose the decedent left enough money to pay for the his funeral and the Probate procedure, with $50,000 left over. If there are no other debts, his beneficiaries will inherit the $50,000.

Suppose instead that he left a hospital bill of $30,000 and a doctor's bill of $30,000 (both Class 4 debts). The $50,000 will be prorated with the hospital getting half and the doctor getting the other half. There will be nothing left to pay any other claim. There will be nothing left for anyone to inherit (Probate 11420 (b)).

There are federal and state laws that set time periods for pursuing a claim. Anyone who wishes to take Court action must do so within the time set by the given Statute of Limitation. For example, a law suit against a health care provider for a wrongful death must be filed within three years of the date of injury or one year after the discovery of the injury, whichever occurs first (Civ. Proc. 340.5).

There is a Statute of Limitations for bringing a claim against the Estate of the decedent. The Personal Representative will give notice to the decedent's creditors of the death, and that a Probate is in progress (Probate 9050, 9052). He will send known creditors notice by mail and publish notice three different times (usually once a week) in a newspaper in the city where the Probate is conducted (Probate 8121). If a creditor fails to file his claim within four months after Letters are issued to the Personal Representative, or within 60 days of receiving written notice (whichever is the later date) his claim is barred (Probate 9100, 9051).

But what if no one starts a Probate procedure? California statute imposes a one year Statute of Limitations from the date of the decedent's death. If a claim is not filed within one year after the death, that claim cannot be enforced against the Estate, the Personal Representative, or any of the beneficiaries. There are exceptions to the one-year limit such as mortgages and federal claims and certain liens on the decedent's property (Civ. Proc. 366.2). But, in general, if no one starts a Probate procedure and a year has passed from the date of the death, the beneficiaries may be able to obtain possession of the decedent's assets free from creditor claims. But read on before you decide to wait out the year.

 **LAWYER**

DECEDENT LEAVING CONSIDERABLE DEBT

If the decedent died leaving much debt and no property, the solution is simple. No Probate, no one gets paid. But if the decedent had property and died owing more money than his property was worth, his heirs may decide that going through Probate is not worth the effort, or they may decide to simply wait out the one year Statute of Limitation period and begin Probate at that time.

This may not be the best decision. Some creditors are tenacious and will use whatever legal strategy is available in order to be paid, including initiating the Probate procedure themselves. If the person named as Executor of the Will does not begin Probate within 30 days from the date of death, the Court may decide that the Executor waived his right to be appointed as Personal Representative (Probate 8001). If a creditor asks to be appointed as Personal Representative at that time, and the Executor cannot give some good reason for the delay, the Court might decide to give the job to the creditor.

As we will see in Chapter 6, a Personal Representative has much authority when conducting the Probate procedure. Family members may object to having a creditor as a Personal Representative, so there could be a court battle over who has priority to be appointed. Court battles are expensive, emotionally as well as financially. Before you decide to distance yourself from the Probate procedure, consult with an attorney experienced in Probate matters for an opinion about the best way to administer the Estate.

MONIES OWED TO THE DECEDENT

Suppose you owed money to the decedent. Do you need to pay that debt now that he is dead? That depends on whether there is some written document that says the debt is forgiven once the decedent dies. For example, suppose the decedent loaned you money to buy your home. If he left a Will saying that once he dies, your debt is forgiven, you do not need to make any more payments. If you signed a promissory note and mortgage at the time you borrowed the money from the decedent, the Personal Representative should sign the original promissory note **PAID IN FULL** and return the note to you.

California law requires that mortgages be released within 30 days of satisfaction. If you do not receive a recorded release, you need to notify the Personal Representative, in writing, that you want the original note and mortgage returned and the mortgage released (Civil 2941). If the mortgage was recorded, the Personal Representative needs to have a *Certificate of Discharge* recorded in the Office of the County Recorder in the county where the mortgage is recorded. You should receive the recorded Certificate of Discharge for your records.

If you signed a Deed of Trust, the Personal Representative, will need to sign whatever documents necessary to reconvey the Deed to you. He should have a *Deed of Reconveyance* recorded in the county where the Deed of Trust is recorded. You should receive the recorded Deed of Reconveyance.

If you owed the decedent money and there is no Will, or if there is a Will, and no mention of forgiving the debt, you still owe the money. Money borrowed from the decedent and his Spouse/RDP needs to be repaid to the Spouse/RDP. Money borrowed from the decedent only, becomes an asset of his Estate.

If you are a beneficiary of his Estate, you may be able to deduct the money from your inheritance. For example, suppose your father left $80,000 to be divided equally between you and your brother. If you owe your father $20,000, your father's Estate is really worth $100,000, with each child entitled to $50,000. Instead of paying the $20,000, you can agree to receive $30,000 and have the $20,000 debt forgiven. Your brother will receive the remaining $50,000.

Who Are The Beneficiaries? 5

A question that comes up early on is who is entitled to the property of the decedent. To answer the question you first need to know how the property was titled (owned) as of the date of death.

There are three ways to own property. The decedent could have owned property jointly with someone, or in trust for another person; or the decedent could have owned property that was titled in his name only.

In general, upon the decedent's death:

Joint Property With Right of Survivorship
belongs to the surviving joint owner.

Trust Property belongs to the beneficiary
of the Trust.

Property owned by the **decedent only**, with no provision for a non-Probate transfer to a beneficiary after death, becomes part of the decedent's Probate Estate to be distributed as part of a Probate procedure.

NOTE ⇨ If the decedent was married or a Domestic Partner his Spouse/RDP may have rights in his property, no matter how it is titled.

This chapter describes each type of ownership in detail.

PROPERTY OWNED JOINTLY

Bank accounts, securities, motor vehicles, real property can all be owned jointly by two or more people. If one of the joint owners dies, then the survivor(s) continue to own their share of the property. Who owns the share belonging to the decedent depends on how the joint ownership was set up.

THE JOINT BANK ACCOUNT

When a bank account is opened the depositors sign an agreement with the bank that states the terms and conditions of the account. If the account is opened in two or more names, the contract will say whether each depositor has authority to make a withdrawal, or whether two signatures are necessary. The statement will also say whether there are is a right of survivorship (Probate 5401).

A joint account is not a survivorship account unless the contract states that the parties have a right of survivorship (Probate 5130). There is no right of survivorship if the account is owned as a Tenancy In Common. In such case, the decedent's share of the account is inherited by the beneficiaries of his Estate.

THE COMMUNITY PROPERTY ACCOUNT

If a couple set up a joint account as Spouse/RDP, it is presumed to be Community Property with each owning half of the account (Probate 5305). The account operates as a Tenancy In Common unless the contract states that there is a right of survivorship. If one of them dies, half of the account belongs to the surviving Spouse/RDP and the remaining half to the Estate of the decedent (Probate 100).

Once an owner of a joint account with right of survivorship dies, the surviving owner is free to withdraw all of the money from the account without the need to go through Probate, but understanding that he may be responsible to pay Estate Taxes on money he inherits from the account (see Chapter 2).

If a joint account with right of survivorship is in three or more names, ownership of a joint account is in proportion to the net contribution of the owners of the account. In the absence of proof otherwise, the parties own an equal share of the account (Probate 5134). Should one owner die, his share is divided equally between the survivors. Of course, any of the surviving owners can go to the bank and withdraw all of the funds. With such an arrangement, the survivors need to cooperate with each other and take only as much of the account as is rightfully theirs.

THE CONVENIENCE ACCOUNT

The decedent may have set up a Convenience Account and given someone (his *Agent*) authority to make bank transactions on his behalf. The Agent dos not own any of the monies in the account, and should not add to or withdraw from the account once the owner of the account dies. The bank will transfer the funds according to the terms of contract or account agreement signed by the decedent.

A bank statement or pass book may not give all of the details of the terms of the bank account, so it is important to actually read the account agreement determine how the account funds should be distributed now that the owner of the account is deceased.

JOINTLY HELD SECURITIES

You can determine whether the decedent owns a security alone or jointly with another by examining the face of the stock or bond certificate. If two names are printed on the certificate followed by a statement that the owners are "Joint Tenants With Right of Survivorship ("JTWRS")," the surviving owner can either cash in the security or ask the company to issue a new certificate in the name of the surviving owner.

Each state has its own securities regulations. If a security held in two or more names was registered or purchased in another state, and it does not indicate whether there is a right of survivorship, you need to contact the company to determine how the account was set up; i.e. with or without survivorship rights.

If the decedent held his securities in a brokerage account, you need to check the monthly or quarterly brokerage statement to see if the account was owned jointly. Not all brokerage firms print the name of a joint owner on the brokerage statement, so you need to contact the brokerage firm and request a copy of the contract that is the basis of the account. It may be that the account is owned jointly, or perhaps the decedent named a beneficiary of the account. If you determine that the account is held jointly or for the benefit of someone, have the brokerage firm forward the necessary forms to transfer the securities to the proper owner or beneficiary.

If a motor vehicle or boat is owned jointly, the name of each owner is printed on the title to the motor vehicle. In California, joint ownership is indicated by the words "AND" or "OR," for example, the title can read: HENRY LEE OR DAVID LEE or the title can read: HENRY LEE AND DAVID LEE which is also written as HENRY LEE/DAVID LEE. These designations have different meanings:

OR The word "OR" means that during the lifetime of the joint owners, either is free to transfer title on his signature alone. Upon the death of one owner, the surviving person owns the car, unless the registration indicate that the car is Community Property or a Tenancy In Common. In such case, the Personal Representative will need to transfer the decedent's "half" of the car to the proper beneficiary.

AND The word "AND" means that both signatures are required to transfer title during their lifetime, however if the title indicates that the car is owned in Joint Tenancy, should one owner die, the other will own the car or boat (Vehicle 4150.5, 9852.5).

MOTOR VEHICLE IN DECEDENT'S NAME ONLY

If the decedent's car/boat was in his name only with a notation on the title to "TRANSFER ON DEATH ('TOD') to a named beneficiary, the beneficiary now owns the vehicle (Vehicle 4150.7, 9852.7). He can have title changed to his name only by taking a death certificate to the nearest Department of Motor Vehicles. The Personal Representative will need to transfer the car/boat to the proper beneficiary, if the decedent owned the car in his name only without such notation, or as Community Property, or as a Tenant in Common. See Chapter 6 for an explanation of how to transfer title to the car.

REAL PROPERTY OWNED JOINTLY

The name of the owner of real property is printed on the face of the deed. To determine whether the decedent owned the property jointly with another person, you need to look at the last recorded deed. The deed will indicate joint ownership. For example:

MICHAEL STONE , a single man, for value received,
hereby grants to
WILLIAM STONE, a single man and
ALICE WASHBURN, a married woman as
JOINT TENANTS
all that real property situated
in the County of San Bernardino, State of California
described as follows . . .

Michael is the **Grantor** of the deed. That means he transferred the property to William and Alice who are the **Grantees** and present owners of the property. The deed states that Alice and Robert are JOINT TENANTS. In California, real property owned as Joint Tenants means that each person owns an equal share of the property and that each has a right of survivorship (Civil 683).

Should either Grantee die, the survivor will own the property 100%. Nothing need be done to establish the ownership, however the decedent's name remains on the deed. An attorney can prepare an **Affidavit of Death of Joint Tenant** for the surviving owner to sign. Once the Affidavit and decedent's death certificate are recorded, the decedent's name is, in effect, removed from the deed.

▤ DEED HELD AS TENANT IN COMMON

If a deed identifies the decedent and another as **TENANTS IN COMMON**, the decedent's share belongs to whomever the decedent named as his beneficiary in his Will. If the decedent died without a Will, the California Laws of Intestate Succession determine who inherits the decedent's share of the property. A Probate proceeding will be necessary to transfer the decedent's share of the property to the proper beneficiary.

If a deed names two or more people as Grantees, but does not state that they own the property:
   "IN JOINT TENANCY" or "AS JOINT TENANTS" or
   "AS JOINT TENANTS WITH RIGHT OF SURVIVORSHIP"
the property is a Tenancy In Common (Civil 683).

 **LAWYER**   THE AMBIGUOUS DEED

Most deeds clearly state whether there are rights of survivorship. But some deeds can be read two ways. For example, suppose a woman deeded her home to herself and her two children as follows:
   Ruth White, Grantor, ... to Ruth White
   jointly with Ralph White and Susan Peters.

Did Ruth intend that they all be joint tenants? Or did she intend that if one of her children died first, that child's share would go to the deceased child's Estate? Best to consult with an attorney if you have any question about how to interpret the deed.

▤ DEED HELD AS SPOUSE/RDP

The decedent may have owned real property together with his Spouse/RDP with or without rights of survivorship. If they owned property as Tenants In Common, and the decedent's share was his Separate Property, it becomes part of his Probate Estate to be distributed as part of a Probate procedure. As we will see in the next Chapter, Probate is not necessary if his share is Community Property, and the surviving Spouse/RDP inherits the decedent's half either as a beneficiary of his Will or according to the Laws of Intestate Succession (Probate 13500). Of course, if the deed identifies the couple as Joint Tenants, the surviving Spouse/RDP owns the property as of the date of death without the need for Probate (Civil 683).

Although the surviving Spouse/RDP owns the Joint Property 100%, only the decedent's half takes a step-up in basis for purposes of the federal Capital Gains Tax law. In other states, a married couple can own property as *Tenants by the Entirety* — with each partner owning the property 100% both before and after death. Should one spouse die, the other takes a step up in basis of the entire value of the property. To address this problem, in 2001, the California legislature created **Community Property With Right of Survivorship** (Civil 682.1, Family 750). If the deed so identifies the property, the surviving spouse inherits the property with a full step-up in basis as of the date of death.

The federal government does not recognize the Domestic Partner relationship, so if the decedent's owned real property together with a Domestic Partner, as Joint Tenants, or as Community Property With Right of Survivorship, only the decedent's half takes a step-up in basis.

▤ DEED WITH A LIFE ESTATE

A *Life Estate* interest in real property means that the person who owns the Life Estate has the right to live in that property until he dies. You can identify a Life Estate interest by examining the face of the deed. If somewhere on the face of the deed you see the phrase RESERVING A LIFE ESTATE to the deceased Grantor, then the Grantee now owns the property. For example, suppose the granting paragraph of the deed reads:

> LEONA SPAULDING, a single woman, . . .
> for consideration paid, grants to,
> FRANKLIN SPAULDING, a married man . . .
> the following described real property
>
> . . .
>
> RESERVING A LIFE ESTATE TO THE GRANTOR

Leona is the owner of the Life Estate. Franklin owns the *Remainder Interest* in the property. Franklin has no right to occupy the property during Leona's lifetime, but once she dies, he will own the property 100%. He will be free to take possession of the property or transfer it, as he sees fit.

As with a survivorship tenancy, nothing need be done to establish Franklin's ownership of the property once Leona dies. However, he may wish to have his attorney record documents showing that he now owns the property.

See Chapter 6 for an explanation of how to transfer real property owned by the decedent.

The laws of the state or country where the property is located determine who inherits property within that state or country. If the decedent owned property in another state or country, regardless of whether he was a resident of California, local law determines who inherits that property.

The laws of each state are similar, but not the same. Laws differ in how the deed needs to be worded in order to have a Right of Survivorship. Some states, like California, do not require the deed to specifically say there is a right of survivorship. In such states, a deed held as Joint Tenant means that there is a right of survivorship, even if the deed does not say so. Other states, require the deed to say whether there is a right of survivorship, and if not, the property is a Tenancy In Common.

The rights of married couples vary significantly. In some states, such as Florida, a Right of Survivorship is created between a married couple merely by having the owners identified as "Husband and Wife." In other states, the deed must state that the married couple have rights of survivorship or that they own the property as "Tenants By The Entirety."

If the decedent owned property in another state, it is important to consult with an attorney in that state to determine who now owns the property.

 THERE COULD BE A LATER DEED

The discussion in this book of the different kinds of ownership of real property assumes that you are in possession of the most recent, valid deed. The decedent could have signed another, later deed. Before you come to a conclusion about who inherits the property, it is advisable to have an attorney or a title insurance company perform a title search to determine the owner of the property as of the decedent's date of death.

PROPERTY HELD IN TRUST

BANK/ SECURITY ACCOUNTS

A bank account or security account that is registered in the name of the decedent "in trust for" or "for the benefit of" someone, will be turned over to the beneficiary once the financial institution has a certified copy of the death certificate. Sometimes the account is called a *Totten Trust* account (Probate 80).

If the beneficiary is a minor, the bank may give the funds to the child's parent, provided the parent signs an *Affidavit* (a sworn, written statement) verifying that the child's total Estate, including the bank account to be transferred, does not exceed $5,000 (Probate 3401). If the account exceeds that value, the funds cannot be transferred without permission from the Probate Court. See Chapter 7 for a discussion of transfers made to minors.

BANK ACCOUNT HELD BY A TRUSTEE

If the bank or security account is registered in the name of the decedent "as Trustee under a Trust Agreement," that means the decedent was the Trustee of a Trust and the bank will turn over that account to the Successor Trustee of the Trust. Banks usually require a copy of the Trust Agreement or a Certificate that identifies the Successor Trustee, so the bank should be aware of the identity of the Successor Trustee. If the Trust was amended to name a different Successor Trustee, you need to present the bank with a copy of that amendment together with a certified copy of the death certificate.

MOTOR VEHICLE

A motor vehicle held in the name of the decedent "as Trustee," continues to be Trust property, so there is no need to change title. However, the Successor Trustee will need to contact the Department of Motor Vehicles to have the car re-registered to his name and address. The Successor Trustee will then dispose of the car according to the terms of the Trust Agreement.

REAL PROPERTY

If the decedent had a Trust and put real property that he owned into the Trust, then the deed may read something like this:

JOHN ZAMORA and MARIA ZAMORA, his wife,
for value received, hereby grant to
JOHN ZAMORA, **Trustee of the**
JOHN ZAMORA REVOCABLE TRUST AGREEMENT
DATED AUGUST 2, 2007
all of that real property situated in
the County of Los Angeles, State of California,
described as follows

. . .

The death of the Trustee of a Trust does not change the ownership of the property. It remains in the Trust. The Trust Agreement might say whether the person who takes John's place as Trustee (the Successor Trustee) should sell or keep the property or perhaps give it to a beneficiary. The Trust may give the Successor Trustee the right to decide what to do with the Trust property. If you are a beneficiary of the Trust and are concerned about what the Successor Trustee will do with the property, you may want to consult with your attorney to learn about your rights under that Trust.

THE DEED OF TRUST

A *Trust Deed* (also known as a *Deed of Trust*) is very different from the above described deed. The Trust Deed is essentially a mortgage. The owner of the property places title to the property with a Trustee as security for payment of monies owed to the lender (Civil 2934a). If the debt is not paid, the Trustee (after proper foreclosure on the property) will deliver title to the property to the beneficiary of the Trust Deed, namely the lender.

PROPERTY IN DECEDENT'S NAME ONLY

If the decedent owned property that was in his name only (not jointly or in trust for someone), some sort of Probate procedure may be necessary in order to transfer the property to the proper beneficiary. Who is entitled to the decedent's Estate depends on whether the decedent died with or without a Will. If he died *testate* (with a valid Will), the beneficiaries of the decedent's property are identified in the Will.

If the decedent died without a valid Will, California's Laws of Intestate Succession determine who inherits the decedent's Probate Estate and what percentage of the Probate Estate each heir is to receive once all the bills and costs of administration are paid.

The law recognizes the right of the family to inherit the decedent's property. The law covers all possible relationships beginning with the decedent's Spouse/RDP. But before we discuss the rights of the surviving Spouse/RDP we need to consider whether that relationship is recognized as valid within state of California.

THE MARITAL RELATIONSHIP

California statute defines marriage to be " . . . a personal relation arising out of a civil contract between a man and a woman, to which the consent of the parties capable of making that contract is necessary. "Consent alone does not constitute marriage. The couple must obtain a license to marry and then solemnize the marriage by a religious or state ceremony (Family 300).

The parties must be at least 18 when they marry; but someone under the age of 18 can marry provided their parent gives written consent AND the Court, after learning all of the facts of the case, issues an order granting them permission to marry (Family 302).

California law does not bar marriages between cousins, however the law prohibits the marriage of those who are:
- ☒ *ancestors* (parent, grandparents, etc.), or *descendants* (child, grandchild, etc.) of each other;
- ☒ brother and sister of the whole or half blood
- ☒ aunt and nephew, or uncle and niece (Family 2200).

☒ BIGAMY

California law also bars the marriage of those who are currently married. A subsequent marriage is not valid unless the former marriage has been dissolved, or the partner has been missing for five successive years or is generally believed to be dead at the time of the subsequent marriage (Family 2201).

THE COMMON LAW MARRIAGE

A Common Law marriage is one that has not been solemnized by ceremony. It is more than just living together. The couple must agree to live together as man and wife, and then publicly hold themselves out as being married; i.e., tell friends, family and business acquaintances that they are married. Many states, including California , no longer recognize a Common Law marriage as being valid. However, if a Common Law marriage is valid in the state where the couple entered into the relationship, that marriage is valid in California as well (Family 308).

SAME SEX MARRIAGES

In 1998, the federal government passed the Defense of Marriage Act, saying that for purposes of federal law, marriage is a legal union between one man and one woman (28 U.S.C. 1738C). But, for purposes of state law, whether you can marry, who you can marry; and how you can marry, are determined by the laws of the state in which you live. There is much variation state to state. Vermont, Connecticut, and New Jersey have approved same-sex *Civil Unions* giving couples the same rights and responsibilities in that state as a married couple. Massachusetts allows gay marriages. The Defense of Marriage Act also provides that no state is required to recognize the laws of another state as relating to same sex marriage. However, under California law, a marriage that is valid in the state where it was contracted (same sex or not) is valid in California (Family 308).

The California legislature has reserved the marital relationship to heterosexual couple, allowing only a man and a woman to obtain a marriage license within the state. None-the-less, they have granted the same rights and responsibilities of a married couple to those who are Registered Domestic Partners (Family 297.5, 308.5).

A Domestic Partner relationship is established by the filing of a *Declaration of Domestic Partner* form with the County Clerk (Family 298). In order to file a Declaration, both persons must be at least 18, not currently in a marital or Domestic Partner relationship, and not related by blood in a way that would prevent their marriage in this state (Family 297). Recognizing that there are elderly people who do not want to jeopardize their Social Security or widow(er) pension by marriage, the statute extended the Domestic Partner registration to heterosexual couples over the age of 62 (Family 297 (5)(B)).

Once the Declaration is signed, the Clerk sends it to the California Secretary of State who then enters the Declaration in the Domestic Partnerships Registry (Family 298.5). The Domestic Partner relationship continues until one partner dies or the relationship is terminated by obtaining a *Dissolution Of Domestic Partnership*. The procedure for the dissolution is much the same as obtaining a Dissolution of Marriage.

The Domestic Partnership can also be terminated by filing a NOTICE OF TERMINATION OF DOMESTIC PARTNERSHIP with the Secretary of State, however this is available only under certain conditions, such as the partnership being registered for less than five years, and no children born or adopted during that time. See statute (Family 299) for the criteria that must be met in order to file a Notice Of Termination of Domestic Partnership with the Secretary of State.

It is important to consult with an at   y
question about the validity of the c   r
Domestic Partner relationship.

If the decedent died without a Will, leaving property in his name only, and without provision for its transfer to a beneficiary, the state provides a Will for him in the form of the *Laws of Intestate Succession*. The distribution of the decedent's Estate depends on who survives him:

✧ SURVIVING DESCENDANT, NO SPOUSE/RDP

If, the decedent was survived by *issue*, i.e., *descendants* (child, grandchild, etc.) and no surviving Spouse/RDP, the decedent's Estate is inherited by his descendants in equal shares (Probate 6402 (a)). If one or more of his children died before him, his Estate is distributed according to California statute (Probate 240).

Probate 240
If a statute calls for property to be distributed or taken in the manner provided in this section, the property shall be divided into as many equal shares as there are living members of the nearest generation of issue then living and deceased members of that generation who leave issue then living, each living member of the nearest generation of issue then living receiving one share and the share of each deceased member of that generation who leaves issue then living being divided in the same manner among his or her then living issue.

If you understood Probate 240 and you are not a lawyer, you missed your calling. For the rest of us (even lawyers) it's a head scratcher. Maybe the easiest way to explain the statute is with an example.

ALL CHILDREN SURVIVE

Suppose the decedent was single with 4 children, Ann, Barry, Carl, David and he died intestate, each child inherits 25% of his estate.

CHILD WITHOUT DESCENDANT DIES BEFORE DECEDENT

If Ann dies before her father, leaving no descendant, Barry, Carl and David divide the Estate between them. Each inherits one-third of the Estate.

CHILDREN WITH DESCENDANT DIES BEFORE DECEDENT

Suppose instead that only Carl and David survived their father. If Ann died leaving no children and Barry died leaving 2 children, the Estate is divided into 3 shares — one for each surviving child (Carl and David) and one share for Barry's children, who divide their share equally.

For simplicity, we will refer to this method of distribution as a **Per Stirpes** distribution (Probate 246).

✧ NO SURVIVING DESCENDANT, SPOUSE/RDP

If the decedent was not survived by a Spouse/RDP, or a descendant, his Estate is distributed equally to his parents. If only one parent survives, (s)he inherits the entire Estate. If there is no surviving parent, his brothers and sisters inherit his Estate, in equal shares, per stirpes. Relatives of half-blood inherit the same as if they were of whole blood. For example, if the decedent had a brother from the same set of parents and a brother with the same father and a different mother, both brothers inherit an equal share (Probate 6406).

If there are no surviving parents, or their descendants, the Estate is inherited by the decedent's surviving grand-parents in equal shares. If there is no surviving grand parent, the Estate is inherited by the decedent's aunts and uncles, in equal shares, per stirpes (Probate 6402).

✧ MARRIED OR A DOMESTIC PARTNER ✧

If the decedent was single the Laws of Intestate Succession apply to all of his *Probate Estate*, i.e., property in his name only, without provision for the transfer of the property after death. If the decedent was married or a Registered Domestic Partner, the Laws of Intestate Succession apply to: ⇨   all of his Separate Property, and

⇨ half of the Community Property (Probate 100).

As explained in the last Chapter, a couple may agree in writing to divide their Community Property differently than that provided by law (Family 852). For purposes of this discussion, we will assume that there is no agreement to divide their Community Property other than 50-50.

✧ SPOUSE/RDP, NO DESCENDANT, NO PARENT, NO SIBLING

The surviving Spouse/RDP inherits the decedent's entire Probate Estate, provided the decedent is not survived by a descendant, parent, brother, sister, or descendant of a brother or sister (Probate 6401 (c)(1)).

✧ SURVIVING SPOUSE/RDP AND DESCENDANT

The Spouse/RDP inherits the decedent's share of their Community Property; i.e., all Community Property now belongs to the Spouse/RDP — but understanding that the Spouse/RDP may need to use that property to pay for money owed by the decedent (See Page 99).

The Spouse/RDP inherits half of the decedent's Separate Property if the decedent has a surviving descendant. The descendant could be a child of the decedent or a child of his deceased child. The Spouse/RDP inherits one third of the decedent's Separate Property if the decedent has more than one descendant (Probate 6401). The descendants inherit the other two-thirds, per stirpes. For example, suppose the decedent is survived by a spouse, child, and two grandchildren of a deceased child.

The spouse now owns all of their Community Property and one-third of his Separate Property. If the descendent left $300,000 in Separate Property, the surviving Spouse/RDP inherits $100,000. The remaining $200,000 is divided into two shares. One share of $100,000 for the surviving child, and one share for the children of the deceased child, who each inherit $50,000.

✧ SPOUSE/RDP, NO DESCENDANT, SURVIVING PARENT OR DESCENDANT OF PARENT

If the decedent was survived by a Spouse/RDP, and he had no surviving descendant, the surviving Spouse/RDP inherits the half of the decedent's Separate Property. The other half is inherited equally by the decedent's parents or the surviving parent. If both parents are deceased, the share goes to the decedent's siblings, in equal shares, per stirpes (Probate 6401(c)(2)(B)).

✧ NO SPOUSE/RDP OR DESCENDANT OF GRANDPARENT

If the decedent was not survived by a Spouse/RDP, descendant, or descendant of his grandparents, but he had a deceased Spouse/RDP, the relatives of the deceased Spouse/RDP may have rights in the Estate, provided the decedent did not remarry or become a RDP after the death of his Spouse/RDP. To inherit the decedent's *real property* (residence, condominium, lot, etc.), the Spouse/RDP must have died within 15 years of the decedent's death. To inherit the decedent's *personal property* (bank account, securities, car, etc., the Spouse/RDP must have died within 5 years of the decedent's death. A death beyond those time limits has no effect on the decedent's Probate Estate. When we refer to a *Deceased Spouse/RDP* in this section, we mean a deceased Spouse/RDP who died within these time limits (Probate 6402.5).

✧ DESCENDANTS OF DECEASED SPOUSE/RDP

If the decedent is not survived by a Spouse/RDP, descendant (child, grandchild, etc.) or a descendant of a grandparent (decedent's parent, sibling, aunt and uncle, or cousin) and he is survived by a Deceased Spouse/RDP, as defined on the previous page, the descendants of the Deceased Spouse inherit the decedent's Estate, in equal shares, per stirpes.

CALIFORNIA: HEIR OF LAST RESORT

Property that is either unclaimed or abandoned, goes to the state; so if the decedent died without a Will and he had absolutely no surviving next of kin, and no surviving kinsfolk of a deceased Spouse/RDP entitled to inherit property under the Laws of Intestate Succession, the decedent's Probate Estate goes to the state of California (Probate 6404).

THE 120 HOUR RULE

A beneficiary must survive the decedent by at least 120 hours for purposes of Intestate Succession. If an heir does not live for at least 120 hours after the decedent's death, the decedent's property is distributed as if the heir died first. This rule does not apply if the imposition of the 120 hour limit results in the state of California inheriting the decedent's property (Probate 6403).

THERE'S MORE

The explanation in this book of California's Laws of Intestate Succession is abridged. There is much more to the Law. Unless the descent is straight forward, with the decedent leaving a surviving Spouse/RDP and/or children (all who survive him), it is best to consult with an attorney before you decide who is entitled to inherit the decedent's Probate Estate.

WHO DIED FIRST?

Sometimes it happens that two family members die simultaneously and no one knows who died first. How is the Estate of each of them distributed in such case? For example, suppose a husband and wife are killed in a car accident. How is their property distributed? As explained, to inherit under the Laws of Intestate Succession, the beneficiary must survive the decedent by at least five days (Probate 6403). If neither had a Will, property belonging to the wife is inherited as if her husband died first, and property belonging to the husband is distributed as if the wife died first. But suppose they had property that is transferred without the need for Probate. In such case, California statute provides for an orderly distribution of property they own jointly with right of survivorship.

JOINTLY OWNED PROPERTY

Property owned by a couple with right of survivorship, with no provision for whom is to inherit the property should they both die, is divided with half going to the Estate of the wife, and the other half to the Estate of the husband. Each half is distributed according to the applicable Will, and if no Will, according to the Laws of Intestate Succession (Probate 223).

LIFE INSURANCE PROCEEDS

Suppose the husband is insured, with his wife as the beneficiary of his life insurance policy. The proceeds of the policy will be distributed as if the wife died before her husband with the proceeds going to the alternate beneficiary named in the policy. If no alternate beneficiary is named, the proceeds of the policy go to the insured party (in this case, the husband's Estate) to be distributed as Community Property (Probate 224). These same rules apply to Domestic Partners who die simultaneously.

THE RIGHTS OF A CHILD

THE NON-MARITAL CHILD

A child born out of wedlock has the same rights to inherit from his/her natural father as does one born in wedlock, provided:

☑ the child is born while his parents are married or within 300 days from the date the marriage was terminated because of divorce, death, legal separation, etc. - or -

☑ the parents marry after the child's birth and with the father's consent, he is identified on the birth certificate as the father - or -

☑ the parents marry after the child's birth and the father is obliged to support the child by signing a voluntary promise to do so, or by Court order - or -

☑ the father takes the child into his home and openly acknowledges the child as his own (Family 7611).

NO SHARE FOR NEGLECTFUL PARENT

Under California law neither the natural parent of a child born out of wedlock, nor any relative of the parent, can inherit the child's property under the Laws of Intestate Succession, unless:

⇨ the parent, or relative of the parent, acknowledges the child AND

⇨ the parent, or relative of the parent, contribute to the support or care of the child (Probate 6452).

Notice this rule does not apply only to fathers. If a mother has a child born out of wedlock, and she does not contribute to that child's support, she can be barred from inheriting from that child under the Laws of Intestate Succession.

THE ADOPTED CHILD

An adopted child has the same right to inherit from an adoptive parent as does a natural child (Probate 6450). The adopted child cannot inherit from a natural parent, unless the adoption took place after the death of one of his parents, or unless the child was adopted by the Spousse/RDP of his natural parent.

The natural parent and the relatives of a natural parent cannot inherit from an adopted child under the California Laws of Intestate Succession with two exceptions:

⇨   whole blood siblings, and their descents, may inherit from the adopted child

⇨   the adoption was by the Spouse/RDP or surviving Spouse/RDP of the natural parent (Probate 6451)

THE FOSTER CHILD, THE STEPCHILD AND THE EQUITABLE CHILD

A foster child and/or stepchild is a "child" for intestate purposes if the relationship with the decedent began before the child was 18 and continued until the death AND evidence shows that there would have been an adoption except for some legal barrier (Probate 6454). Similarly, a Court can find that a child was "equitably" adopted if some special circumstance justifies that conclusion (Probate 6455).

THE AFTERBORN CHILD

A child who was conceived prior to the decedent's death, and born to the surviving spouse after the death, has the same right to inherit as any other natural child of the decedent (Probate 6407).

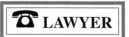

NO SHARE FOR KILLER OR ABUSER

Under California law, anyone who is found to be guilty of intentionally killing the decedent, is prohibited from profiting from the crime. Property that the killer would have inherited as a beneficiary of the decedent's Will or Trust is distributed as if the killer died before the decedent (Probate 250).

☎ LAWYER — LAW SUIT FOR WRONGFUL DEATH

If anyone caused an injury to the decedent that was related to his death, regardless of whether that person is convicted of a crime, the Personal Representative may sue that person for a wrongful death on behalf of those entitled to inherit his Estate under the Laws of Intestate Succession (Civ. Proc. 377.60). See page 25 for a discussion of a wrongful death.

NO SHARE FOR ABUSER

Sometimes an elderly person is not killed but is physically or financially abused. If an elderly or a dependent person is abused and later dies, the abuser may not profit from the death, provided <u>all</u> of the following can be proven:

⇨ The abuser was found guilty of physical or financial abuse.

⇨ The abuser acted with bad faith.

⇨ The abuser committed acts of abuse in a reckless, oppressive, fraudulent or malicious manner.

⇨ The victim was unable to manage his finances or resist fraud or undue influence from the time the acts occurred up to the time he died (Probate 259).

If the decedent left a valid Will, directions for distributing his property are given in the Will. Most Wills are short and easy to read, however, you may come across an unfamiliar legal term such as the term *per capita*, for example:

"I leave the rest, residue and remainder of my property to my children, Robert, Barry and Carl, in equal shares, <u>per capita</u>."

This means that if one child dies before the decedent, then the share intended for that child is to be shared equally by the surviving brothers.

This is different than a *per stirpes* distribution, for example:

"I leave the rest, residue and remainder of my property to my children, Robert, Barry and Carl, in equal shares, <u>per stirpes</u>."

In this case if one of the beneficiaries dies, his share will be shared equally by the children of the beneficiary, i.e., by the Will maker's grandchildren (Probate 240). See page 140 for an explanation of a per stirpes distribution.

Sometimes a Will is ambiguous and can be read in different ways. In such case, it may be necessary to have the Probate Court decide what the decedent intended.

In the next few pages we examine different problems that can arise when offering a Will into Probate, and when to consider challenging the validity of the Will.

It is not uncommon for a family member to be unhappy with the way the decedent willed his property. If you are tempted to challenge a Will, first consider whether the Will is valid under California law. In California, a Will is presumed valid if at the time the decedent made the Will he was at least 18, and of *sound mind* (Probate 6100).

Under California law, a Will maker is considered to be of sound mind at the time he made the Will if:

- ☑ he knew what he was doing

  (namely making a Will), AND
- ☑ he knew what property he had, AND
- ☑ he remembered his family and how they would be affected by his Will, AND
- ☑ he was not suffering from a delusional mental disorder affecting his ability to distribute his property (Probate 6100.5).

The first step in the Probate proceeding is to have the Court determine whether the Will presented is valid. There should be no problem in having the Will accepted into Probate, if it is in writing and signed by the Will maker in the presence of at least two credible witnesses. If the signatures on the Will are notarized, and no one contests the Will, the Court will consider the Will to be *self-proved*, and not require further proof of its authenticity (Probate 8220). If the Will is witnessed but not notarized, the Court may ask the witnesses to testify that they saw the Will maker sign the Will, and he was at least 18 and of sound mind when he did so.

But suppose the decedent wrote out a Will in his own hand and signed it with no one present?

☒ THE UNWITNESSED WILL

A Will written in the Will maker's hand is called a **holographic Will**. California allows a holographic Will (witnessed or unwitnessed) to be admitted to Probate provided the signature and the material parts of the Will (the date and the "who" gets "what") are in the Will maker's own hand (Probate 6111).

The problem with an unwitnessed holographic Will is its authenticity. Because no one saw the decedent sign the Will, it is hard to determine whether the Will was written by the decedent or is a forgery. If the Will is challenged, no doubt each side will bring in their own handwriting experts who will support their position of whether the decedent did, or did not, sign the Will. If the decedent left an unwitnessed holographic Will, you should consult with an attorney experienced in Probate matters.

☒ THE WILL WITNESSED BY A BENEFICIARY

Having two witnesses usually solves the problem of its authenticity; but if either witness is a beneficiary of the will, the Court will presume that the witness got that gift by using duress, menace, fraud or undue influence. Although the law presumes the gift was made because of improper actions on the part of the witness, the witness will get the gift unless someone challenges the Will and the Court hears evidence to prove that such was in fact the case. If the challenge is successful, the witness will receive as much as he would have received under the Laws of Intestate Succession (Probate 6104, 6112).

For example, suppose the decedent is survived only by a son and daughter. If his Will gives his entire Estate to his son, and his son was the only witness to the Will, the daughter may challenge the Will on the basis of Probate 6112. If the daughter is successful, the son will receive half of the Estate and the daughter the other half.

☒ UNDUE INFLUENCE

Even if the Will was signed in the presence of two disinterested witnesses, it could be that the Will is challenged because someone is accused of pressuring the decedent into giving him most, if not all, of his property. California courts have ruled that to prove **undue influence,** whoever makes the challenge needs to prove that:

⇨ there was a confidential relationship between the decedent and the beneficiary (close relative, spiritual advisor, attorney, doctor, financial advisor, etc.) AND

⇨ the beneficiary actively worked to get the decedent to sign the Will (*Estate of Callahan,* 67 Cal.2d 609 (1967); 423 P.2d 963).

California law prohibits the lawyer who drafted the Will from inheriting anything under that Will. Not only is the lawyer prohibited from making gifts to himself, he is also prohibited from including gifts in the Will to anyone in his law firm, his Spouse/RDP, or anyone else related to him through blood or marriage (Probate 21350).

☒ THE VERBAL WILL

Picture a death bed scene. The elderly gentleman is surrounded by several family members. In a whisper, just audible enough to be heard, he says: "Even though I am a wealthy man, I never got around to making a Will. You all have been good to me, but I did want my entire fortune to go to my nephew, Robert. He has been like a son to me. "
Do you think Robert can inherit his Uncle's Estate?
Not in California unless:

⇨ someone writes down his uncles's wishes, AND

⇨ the uncle acknowledges that this is his Will, AND

⇨ the uncle signs the Will, or has someone sign for him, in his presence, and at his direction, AND

⇨ the Will is witnessed and signed by at least two persons each of whom were present at the time he made the Will and who understood that the document they signed as witnesses is the Uncle's Will (Probate 6110).

Considering that the uncle's relatives will probably inherit the fortune under California's Laws of Intestate Succession, it is doubtful that Robert is in danger of becoming wealthy at any time in the near future.

WHEN TO CHALLENGE A WILL
If you can prove the decedent was under 18 when he signed the Will, you have it made. Challenging the Will on other grounds may be difficult — especially if the Will was prepared by the decedent's attorney, who will, no doubt, testify that the Will maker's mind was perfectly clear when he signed the document; and that he signed it of his own free will. But difficult is not impossible. If you are concerned about the validity of the Will, it is important to consult with an attorney experienced in Probate litigation.

☒ THE WILL THAT IS CONTRARY TO LAW

Sometimes a person who is of sound mind, makes a Will, but that Will has the effect of giving a spouse or a minor child less than is required under California law. One such example is that of Nancy. Hers was not an easy life. She worked long hours as a waitress. She divorced her hard drinking first husband. The final judgment gave her their homestead, some securities, and sole custody of their son. After the divorce, Nancy had her attorney prepare a Will leaving all she owned to her son, Richard.

Some years later she met and married Harry, a chef at the restaurant where she worked. He moved into her home and they later had a daughter. Richard was 21, and his half-sister 15, when Nancy died after a lengthy battle with cancer.

Nancy did not leave much — her car, her home, and the securities worth about $70,000, all were in Nancy's name only. She had a small checking account that she held jointly with her son Richard. Before she died, she told Richard, that she had not changed her Will because she wanted him to have all she owned. She said Harry had a good job and she was sure he would take good care of his daughter.

No sooner was the funeral over, when stepson came in and demanded that Harry vacate his mother's home and give him the keys to her car.

Harry was furious and went to his attorney.

"I was a good husband to Nancy, supporting and taking care of her all during her illness. It was me, and not her son who was at her side when she died. Now Richard is trying to put me out in the street and take the keys to her car. Can he do that ?"

The attorney reassured him. "No. Under California law, you and your daughter have the right to continue to live in the home at least until the Probate proceeding is over. You can even ask the judge to allow you to continue living there until your daughter is 18 (Probate 6523, 6524). As for the car, if Nancy purchased it with money she earned after the marriage, it is Community Property and it now belongs to you. Nancy married you after she made her Will, so under California law you have the right to inherit her Community Property and as much of her Separate Property as you would have inherited had she died without a Will — but not more than half of her Separate Property (Probate 21610). Nancy had two children, so you are entitled to one-third of the value of her Separate Property. These are your rights under California law unless you *waived* them by signing a Premarital or Marital Agreement (Probate 141, 6401, 21611)."

"No, I never signed anything. What about my daughter. Doesn't she have any rights?"

"She sure does. California law provides that a child born after a Will is made is entitled to a share of the Estate equal to what she would have inherited had her mother died without a Will (Probate 21620). That means she is entitled to a one-third share of her mother's Separate Property. In addition, you can ask the judge to award you a Family Allowance for your daughter's maintenance during the Probate (Probate 6540)."

Richard did not fare as well as his mother intended. The judge found the car to be Community Property and awarded it to Harry. The judge ordered that Harry and his daughter be allowed to occupy the Nancy's home until the daughter turned 18. He awarded a Family Allowance for the daughter's support during the Probate administration.

The securities had to be sold to pay for the funeral expenses, medical bills, the Family Allowance, and the cost of Probate. All that Richard inherited was his one-third share of the house. And he didn't get that until it was sold three years later.

No doubt Nancy did not understand what would happen to her Estate once she passed on. The Will she left did not accomplish her goal of providing for her son. All it did was cause turmoil and an irreparable rift between Harry and Richard. It didn't need to be that way. Had Nancy known about California law, she could have consulted with an attorney and set up an Estate Plan that could have provided for her son without alienating her husband.

But the moral of the story, for the purpose of this discussion, is that if you believe that the decedent's Will is not valid or is not drafted according to California law, you need to consult with an attorney experienced in Probate matters to determine your legal rights under that Will.

Getting Possession Of The Property 6

Knowing who is entitled to receive the decedent's property is one thing. Getting that property is another. As explained in the previous chapter, if the decedent owned property jointly with another, or in trust for someone, the property now belongs to the surviving joint owner or the beneficiary of the Trust.

If the decedent owned a joint bank account, the surviving joint owner is free to withdraw all of the money in the account. However, as explained in Chapter 4, whoever withdraws the money needs to keep in mind that the decedent's share of the account might be needed to pay Estate Taxes.

If the decedent owned real or personal property in his name only, or if he owned property as a Tenant In Common, some sort of Probate will be necessary in order to transfer ownership to the proper beneficiary. This chapter describes the different kinds of Probate procedures that are available in California and when it is appropriate to use that procedure.

You may need to employ an attorney should a full Probate administration be necessary, but there are many items that can be transferred without the need for Probate. This chapter explains how to get possession of such items.

Too often, the first person to discover the body will help himself to the decedent's *personal effects* (clothing, jewelry, appliances, electrical equipment, cameras, books, stamp or coin collection, household items and furnishing, etc.). Unless that person is the decedent's sole beneficiary, such action is unconscionable, if not illegal.

The decedent's Spouse/RDP, or if no Spouse/RDP, his minor children can ask the Court to keep certain of his possessions free of creditor's claim (Civ. Proc. 703.140, Probate 6510, 6520). Those items are listed on page 115. All other personal property should be given to whom-ever is appointed as Personal Representative to be distributed according to the decedent's Will, or if no Will according to California's Laws of Intestate Succession.

All the rest of the decedent's personal effects need to be given to the Personal Representative to be distributed as part of the Probate proceeding. If Probate is not necessary, whoever is next of kin according to the Laws of Intestate Succession may keep the decedent's personal effects. If two or more people are entitled to the property, they need to divide it in approximately equal proportions among themselves.

What's Equal?

The decedent's personal property may need to be divided equally between two or more next or kin, or the decedent's Will may direct that two or more beneficiaries share a gift "equally." The problem with the term "equal" is that people have different ideas of what "equal" means.

Unless there is clear evidence that the decedent's Will meant something else, "equal" refers to the monetary value of the item and not to the number of items received. For example, to divide the decedent's personal effects equally, one beneficiary may receive an expensive item of jewelry and another beneficiary may receive several items whose overall value is approximately equal to that single piece of jewelry.

When distributing personal effects there needs to be cooperation and perhaps compromise, or else bitter arguments might arise over items of little monetary value. One such argument occurred when an elderly woman died who was rich only in her love for her five children and ten grandchildren. After the funeral, the children gathered in their mother's apartment. Each child had his/her own furnishings and no need for anything in the apartment. They agreed to donate all of their mother's personal effects to a local charity with the exception of a few items of sentimental value.

Each child took some small item as a remembrance — a handkerchief, a large platter that their mother used to serve family dinners, a doily their mother crocheted. Things went smoothly until it came to her photograph album. Frank, the youngest sibling, said, "I'll take this." Marie objected saying "But there are pictures in that album that I want."

Frank retorted, "You already took all the pictures Mom had on her dresser."

The argument went downhill from there. Unsettled sibling rivalries boiled over, fueled by the hurt of the loss that they were all experiencing. It almost came to blows when the eldest settled the argument: "Frank, you make copies of all of the photos in the album for Marie. Marie, you make copies of all of the pictures that you took and give them to Frank. This way you both will have a complete set of Mom's pictures. And while you're at it, make copies for the rest of us."

NON-PROBATE TRANSFERS

A *non-Probate transfer* is a transfer of the decedent's property without the need for Probate. For example, if the decedent had a bank account in his name only "In Trust For" someone or with instructions to "Pay On Death" to someone, all the beneficiary need do is produce a death certificate and proper identification, and the bank will turn over the property to the beneficiary (Probate 5302). Securities that are held jointly with someone, or with instructions to "Transfer On Death" to a named beneficiary, can be transferred to that beneficiary in the same manner (Probate 5507).

An account owned jointly with a Spouse/RDP is presumed to be Community Property. The account should say whether there is a right of survivorship. If there is a right of survivorship, the Spouse/RDP is free to close out the account without going through Probate. Without a right of survivorship, the decedent's half is transferred according to his Will or by the laws relating to Community Property (Probate 5203).

TRANSFERRING THE MOTOR VEHICLE

Probate is not necessary to transfer a car to the surviving joint owner who has rights of survivorship, or to the named beneficiary of a TOD designation (Vehicle 4150.7). The surviving owner can go to the nearest Department of Motor Vehicles ("DMV") and transfer the car to his name only. He can do this on his signature alone, unless there is a lien on the car. If money is owed, title to the car cannot be changed until the lien is released.

A motor vehicle can be transferred to the proper beneficiary without the need for Probate, provided:
⇨   the car is registered in the state of California
⇨   at least 40 days have passed since the date of death
⇨   the beneficiary signs an **Affidavit for Transfer Without Probate (REG 5)** verifying that no one else has a right to the car.
You can download the form from the Department of Motor Vehicles Web. http://www.dmv.ca.gov
You can call the DMV at (800) 777-0133 to determine the cost of the transfer and what documents they require.

If Probate is necessary, it is the Personal Representative's job to transfer the car to the proper beneficiary. If the Will makes a *specific gift* of the car, the Personal Representative will transfer the car to that person. If there was no mention of the car in his Will, or the decedent died without a Will, it becomes part of the *Residuary Estate*, i.e., whatever is left once bills, taxes, costs of administration have been paid and special gift distributed. The Personal Representative may decide to sell the car and distribute the proceeds to the *residuary beneficiaries* of the Estate; or he can transfer the car to one of the beneficiaries as part of that beneficiary's inheritance.

TRANSFER WHEN MORE THAN ONE BENEFICIARY

If there is more than one person who has the right to inherit the car, they all can take title to the car. That may not be a practical thing to do since only one person can drive the car at any given time and if one gets into an accident, they all can be held liable. The better route is for the beneficiaries to agree to have one person take title to the car. The person taking title will need to compensate the others for their share of the car. In such case the beneficiaries need to come to an agreement as to the value of the car.

DETERMINING THE VALUE OF THE CAR

Cars are valued in different ways. The *collateral* value of the car is the value that banks use to evaluate the car for purposes of making a loan to the owner of the car. If you were to trade in a car for the purpose of purchasing a new one, the car dealer would offer you its *wholesale* value. Were you to purchase that same car from a car dealer, he would price it at its *retail* or *fair market value*. Usually the retail price is highest, wholesale is lowest and its collateral value is somewhere in between.

You can call your local bank to get the collateral value of the car. It may be more difficult to obtain the wholesale value because the amount of money a dealer is willing to pay depends on the value of the new car that you are purchasing. You can determine the car's retail value by looking at comparable used car advertisements in the local newspaper. Rather than going through the effort of determining these three values, you can visit the Kelly Blue Book Web site. It gives Low, Average and High Blue Book Values, which in general, corresponds to the wholesale, collateral and retail values.

KELLY BLUE BOOK
http://www.kbb.com

Once the fair market value of the car is determined, the beneficiary who takes the car will be considered to have received that value as part of his inheritance. If none of the beneficiaries want the car, the Personal Representative will sell it and add the proceeds to the amount distributed to the beneficiaries.

MAKING THE TRANSFER

It is important to change title to any motor vehicle owned by the decedent as soon as you are able. If you are the surviving joint owner, you might be able to get a reduced insurance rate if only one person is insured under the policy. It is a good idea to limit the use of the car until it is sold or transferred to the beneficiary. If the decedent's car is involved in an accident before the car is transferred to the new owner, the decedent's Estate may be liable for the damage. Having adequate insurance on the car may save the Estate from monetary loss, but a pending lawsuit could delay Probate and prevent any money from being distributed to the beneficiaries until the lawsuit is settled.

If you are the Personal Representative and are selling the car, or transferring it to a beneficiary, you may want to accompany the beneficiary to the DMV to transfer the vehicle. You will need Court authorization to make the transfer. In most cases, such authorization is included as part of your Letters. In other cases, it will be a separate Court order.

The beneficiary needs to apply for his own Certificate of Title and Registration. He has up to 10 days from the date of transfer to do so. You, as Personal Representative, are responsible to file a **NOTICE OF TRANSFER AND RELEASE OF LIABILITY** with the DMV within 5 days of the transfer.

CANCEL THE DECEDENT'S DRIVER'S LICENSE

It is important to notify the Department of Motor Vehicles of the death. You can turn in the decedent's driver's license when you transfer the motor vehicle to the new owner. If the decedent was disabled and had a parking placard or license plate, those items need to be cancelled as well. The decedent may not have owned a motor vehicle, but he still could have had a driver's licence or a Photo Identification Card. Enclose the card with the word "DECEASED" written on its face together with a certified copy of the death certificate and take it to the nearest DMV office or mail it to:

DEPARTMENT OF MOTOR VEHICLES
REGISTRATION OPERATIONS
P.O. Box 942869
Sacramento, CA   94269-0001

Once notified, the Department will take the decedent off of its mailing list. This will assist the Department in preventing others from using the decedent's name for fraudulent purposes.

CANCEL THE DECEDENT'S VOTER REGISTRATION CARD

In 1993, the federal government passed the National Voter Registration Act requiring states to offer voter registration at public assistance agencies including the Department of Motor Vehicles (42 U.S.C. 1973gg-2). You can ask the DMV to have the Election Board remove the decedent's name from the list of voters at the same time you cancel his driver's license. If the decedent did not have a driver's license, you can contact the Election Board in the county of his residence for information about how to cancel his voter registration. This will help the Election Board in preventing others from using the decedent's name for fraudulent purposes.

The leased car is not an asset of the Estate because the decedent did not own the car. The decedent was obligated to pay the balance of the monies owed on the lease agreement, so the car is a liability to the Estate. The Personal Representative needs to work out an agreement with the company to either assign the lease to someone who agrees to pay the balance of the lease — or have the Estate pay off the lease by purchasing the car under the terms of the lease agreement.

Some lenders will allow the lease to be assigned provided the Estate remains liable for the balance of payment. In such cases, it is better to have the car refinanced and have the original lease paid in full.

If the remaining payments exceed the current market value of the car, there may be a temptation to hand the keys over to the leasing company. This may not be the best strategy, because the leasing company can sell the car and then sue the Estate for the balance of the monies owed. If the decedent had no assets or if his only assets are creditor proof, simply returning the car may be an option. But if the decedent's Estate has assets available to pay the balance of the lease payments, the Personal Representative needs to arrange to have the car transferred in a way that releases the Estate from all further liability.

As explained in Chapter 3, a mobile home that is motorized and not permanently attached to real property is considered to be personal property (Health & Safety 18010). Like any motor vehicle it is titled and registered with the Department of Motor Vehicles. The beneficiary of the mobile home will need to have it titled and registered in the same manner as just described.

A manufactured home, mobile home, house trailer or trailer coach that is used for residential purposes and permanently attached to the land, or connected to utility, water, or sewerage facilities is considered to be an improvement to real property. As with any other house on a parcel of land, it is assessed and taxed to the owner of the land.

Several things need to be done before the Mobile/Manufactured home is sold or transferred to a beneficiary. If there is a loan on the home, the lender must agree to the transfer. Unless the decedent made provision for payment of the loan, the beneficiary of the home will need to arrange to either pay off the loan, or refinance the property.

Before transferring the Mobile/Manufactured home, you need to find whether the land on which the mobile home is located was leased or owned by the decedent. If the decedent was renting space in a trailer park, contact the trailer park owner to transfer the lease agreement to the beneficiary of the mobile home. If the decedent owned the land under the mobile home, the house and the land need to be transferred to the proper beneficiary. Title to the home is transferred as personal property. Title to the land is transferred as described later in this chapter. Hopefully, the beneficiary of the home and the beneficiary of the land are the same person.

If not, the beneficiary of the Mobile/Manufactured home will need a lease agreement with the beneficiary of the land. If the beneficiary of the land refuses to lease the space, the beneficiary of the Mobile/Manufactured home will need to arrange to move it to a trailer park, or to land that he owns.

If you are the new owner of the Mobile/Manufactured home and you wish to move the home, you will need to comply with the regulations as stated in Health & Safety Code 18551. You will need to notify the County Assessor and the **Department of Housing and Community Development** at least 30 days prior to the move. You can call the Department of Housing at (916) 445-4782 for information about consents and licenses you will need in order to move the home.

TRANSFERRING WATERCRAFT

All motor boats and sailboats that exceed 8' in length must be registered with the Department of Motor Vehicles ("DMV"). If the boat was owned jointly or had a TOD designation, the beneficiary may transfer title in the same manner as any motor vehicle with such designation (Vehicle 9852.7). If title was in the decedent's name only, the Personal Representative will issue a bill of sale to the beneficiary. The new owner needs to obtain his own registration by completing an application for Vessel Certificate of Number, form **BOAT 101**. He can obtain the application form from the nearest DMV office or he can download **BOAT 101** from the DMV Web site. http://www.dmv.ca.gov.

Vessels registered in California are assessed property taxes by the County Tax Collector where the boat is moored. The Personal Representative needs to verify that taxes on the boat are paid up to the date of transfer and to notify the County Tax Collector of the change of ownership.

If the decedent owned an aircraft, the Personal Representative will need to arrange to transfer title to the proper beneficiary. The aircraft needs to be titled and registered with the Civil Aviation Registry of the Federal Aviation Administration ("FAA").

FAA REGISTRATION

If you are the new owner of the decedent's aircraft you need to register it with the FAA AIRCRAFT REGISTRATION BRANCH. You will need to

⇨ complete an Aircraft Registration Application (AC FORM 8050-1)

⇨ show proof of ownership, such as a bill of sale

⇨ pay the registration fee.

Call the Registration Branch at (405) 954-3116 or toll free (866) 762-9434 for a copy of the Registration Application or download the form from the FAA Website.

http://www.faa.gov/

California does not register aircraft, but they do tax planes as personal property. The Assessor of the county where the aircraft is usually located is in charge of assessing the plane at its market value. The Personal Representative needs to notify the County Tax Assessor of the change of ownership. He will need to identify the aircraft by its make, model, and aircraft registration number (Rev. & Tax 5362, 5366, 5391).

THE FEDERAL INCOME TAX REFUND

Any refund due to the decedent under a joint federal income tax return filed by his surviving spouse will be sent to the surviving spouse. If the decedent's Personal Representative filed the final return, the refund check will be sent to him to be deposited in the Estate account.

If the decedent was single and Probate is not necessary, whoever is entitled to the decedent's Estate is entitled to the refund check. If you are the beneficiary of the decedent's Estate, you can obtain the refund by filing IRS form 1310 along with the decedent's final income tax return (the 1040). You can obtain form 1310 from the decedent's accountant, or if he did not have an accountant and you wish to file yourself, you can call the IRS at (800) 829-3676 to obtain the form.

You can download instructions, publications and forms from the Internal Revenue Service by going to the FORMS AND PUBLICATIONS section of their Web site.

INTERNAL REVENUE SERVICE
http://www.irs.gov/

The Personal Representative does not need to file form 1310 because once he files the decedent's final income tax return, any refund will be forwarded to him. Similarly, it is not necessary for the surviving spouse who filed a joint return to file form 1310.

If you have not yet received the refund, you can check on it by calling (800) 829-4477, or by visiting the IRS Web site.

As explained in Chapter 2, the decedent's final California income tax return needs to be filed at the same time the federal income tax return is filed (Rev. & Tax 18566). If the decedent was married, the surviving Spouse/RDP may file a joint return with the decedent's Personal Representative signing for the decedent (Rev. & Tax 18524). If Probate is not necessary, the surviving Spouse/RDP may file a joint return on his/her own signature. If the decedent was single the sole beneficiary of the decedent's Estate may file the final return. If you have any question about filing the final state income tax return, call the California Taxpayer Advocate at (800) 852-5711. Out of state, call (916) 845-6600.

If a refund is due, and you wish to check on its status , call the above number, or check the status at the Web site of the Franchise Tax Board.

http://www.ftb.ca.gov

DEPOSITING THE TAX REFUND

If the Personal Representative filed the state income tax return, the check will be mailed to him, to be deposited to the Estate account. If you are the surviving spouse and you filed a joint return prior to the death, you may deposit the check to your joint account. If you do not have a joint account and the bank refuses to cash the check, call the above number and ask the Board for a letter authorizing the bank to cash the check.

If they still refuse, you can write to the Board and ask them to issue a new check in your name only.

FRANCHISE TAX BOARD
P.O. BOX 942840
Sacramento, CA 94240-0040

If all of the decedent's property is inherited by his Spouse/RDP, the Spouse/RDP can ask the Court to issue an order stating that no administration is necessary and that all of the property described in the order be transferred to the Spouse/RDP.

Before issuing an order the Court will want to know all of the facts of the case:

⇨ whether there was a valid Will, and if so, who was named as Executor

⇨ the name, age, address and relationship of anyone who might have a right to inherit the property

⇨ whether there was any written agreement between the decedent and his Spouse/RDP regarding the division of their property (Probate 13650, 13651).

Obtaining the order is much simpler than Probate, but it does require going before the Court and presenting the information to the judge so that he is satisfied that the statute applies.

An order to distribute the Estate is available even if not all of the property goes to the Spouse/RDP. Regardless of whether you seek an order for some or all of the Probate Estate, it is best to consult with an attorney experienced in Probate matters to assist in obtaining the order. If you try to get the order without the assistance of an attorney, and the judge denies the order, it might cost you more in time and money than if you had consulted with an attorney in the first place.

LAST PAYCHECK TO SPOUSE/DP

The decedent's last paycheck can be collected by whoever is appointed as Personal Representative. If Probate is not necessary, the surviving Spouse/RDP has the right to collect up to $5,255** of the decedent's unpaid wages, including compensation for unused vacation. The $5,255 limit does not apply to the surviving Spouse/RDP of a California fire fighter or peace officer (Probate 13600).

**This is the 2007 value. As of 1/1/2003 (and each January 1st there after) the initial statutory amount of $5,000 is adjusted up to 1% for the cost of living.

At any time after the death, the surviving Spouse/RDP can get the decedent's last paycheck by giving the decedent's employer an Affidavit, (i.e., a written statement, sworn to before a Notary Public) verifying that:

☑ As the decedent's Spouse/RDP, the *Affiant* (the person signing the Affidavit) is entitled to the decedent's last pay check, and no one else has a right to his earnings.

☑ No Probate proceeding is being, or has been conducted in California.

☑ The Affiant has not collected, nor is (s)he trying to collect compensation in excess of $5,255.

☑ All of the items to be included in the Affidavit are set out in Probate Code 13601.

Once the employer receives an Affidavit prepared according to Probate Code 13601, he is required to give the last paycheck to the Spouse/RDP. If he fails to do so, the Spouse/RDP can either start a Probate proceeding and have the Personal Representative transfer the funds, or sue the employer for the money. If the Spouse/RDP sues, and the Court finds that the employer acted unreasonably, he will be required to pay all attorney's fees and costs (Probate 13604).

The decedent's Spouse/RDP can get the decedent's last paycheck (provided it is $5,255 or less) by simply giving the employer an Affidavit. An Affidavit can also be used to transfer personal property owned by the decedent, provided the *Gross Value* of property he owns in this state is $100,000 or less. The Gross Value includes all of his real and personal property located in California, but not including property identified in Code 13050, namely:

⇨ his boats, motor vehicles or mobile home

⇨ salary due to him up to $5,255, and any amount due to him for service in the U.S. armed forces

⇨ property he owned jointly with another or which his Spouse/RDP inherits without the need for Probate

⇨ other property that can be transferred without the need for Probate, such as a Pay On Death account, or property in which he held a Life Estate interest, or property in the decedent's Revocable Living Trust (Probate 13100).

The Gross Value includes real property owned by the decedent in California that was titled in his name only or as a Tenant In Common; however the realty must be appraised by a **Probate Referee**, i.e., an appraiser appointed by the Probate Court (Probate 13103). In such case, it may be just as easy to go through Probate.

The use of an Affidavit is appropriate if all that needs to be transferred is personal property (stocks, bonds, bank accounts, etc.) whose value does not exceed $100,000. Probate Code 13101 gives all of the things that must be included in the Affidavit. A sample Affidavit appears on the next page.

AFFIDAVIT FOR TRANSFER OF PERSONAL PROPERTY PURSUANT TO PROBATE CODE 13101

Affiant declares that the following is true:

1. The decedent _____ died on _____ (date) at the county of _____ state of _____.

2. At least 40 days have elapsed since the date of death as shown in the certified copy of the death certificate of the decedent which is attached to this Affidavit.

3. No proceeding is now being or has been conducted in California for administration - or - if commenced the Personal Representative has consented in writing to the use of this procedure.

4. The current gross fair market value of the decedent's real and personal property, excluding property described in Section 13050 of the California Probate Code, does not exceed $100,000.

5. The following is a description of the property of the decedent that is to be paid, transferred, or delivered to affiant or declarant:_____

6. Affiant is the successor of the decedent and to the decedent's interest in the described property, and no other person has a superior right to the interest of the decedent in the property.

7. Affiant requests that the described property be paid, delivered or transferred to the affiant.

I affirm or declare, under penalty of perjury under the laws of the State of California, that the foregoing is true and correct.

Affiant Name _____ Signature _____ date _____

Signed at _____ County, State of _____

_____
Notary Signature and Seal

Is This Too Good To Be True?

This seems almost too easy. The reader may be thinking "You mean that all I need to do is go to a brokerage office, or bank, give them an Affidavit and they will hand over the decedent's personal property?" The answer is "Yes, but..."

▶ YOU NEED TO PRODUCE IDENTIFICATION ◀

The law requires the person in possession of the decedent's property to be reasonably certain of your identity, so you will need to produce a passport, driver's license, an identification card issued by the DMV, or any branch of the armed forces (Probate 13104).

▶ YOU NEED EVIDENCE OF OWNERSHIP ◀

You need to produce evidence that the decedent owned the object in question. For example, if you are having a stock, bond or Certificate of Deposit transferred, you need to produce the original certificate. If you do not have the certificate, the person in possession of the property can require that you post bond to protect him from any loss in the event that you do not have the right to take the property (Probate 13102).

▶ THE TRANSFER CAN BE REFUSED ◀

The person in possession of the property might refuse to accept the Affidavit from anyone other than a Court appointed Personal Representative. In such case, you can either go through the Probate procedure, or you can sue the person in possession to compel the transfer. If the Court finds that the person in possession acted unreasonably, not only do you get the property, you also get your attorney's fees (Probate 13105).

▶ YOU ARE LIABLE FOR DECEDENT'S DEBTS ◀

If you use an Affidavit to take the decedent's property and money is owed on the item, you become liable to pay money owed on that item (Probate 13109). For example, if the decedent took out a bank loan of $25,000 and used his $50,000 Certificate of Deposit as collateral, you need to pay the $25,000 before you can get the CD. If the CD was not used to secure any debt, but the decedent owed money to creditors, by taking the CD you make yourself personally liable for any of the decedent's unsecured debts, up to the value of the fair market value of the item you took.

Creditors have a year to come forward and demand payment from you (Civ. Proc. 366.2). The period of liability reduces to four months if a Personal Representative has been appointed and he has given notice to the creditors according to California statute (Probate 9100). But if a Personal Representative is appointed, you will not be able to use an Affidavit unless he gives you permission to do so. Even if the Personal Representative gives you permission, he can later require that you return the item to the Estate if it is needed to pay the decedent's debts, (Probate 13111). If that happens and you no longer have the item, you will need to reimburse the Estate for its fair market value together with as much interest as the law allows on a money judgment (10% as of the year 2007) (Civ. Proc. 685.010).

If you use an Affidavit to obtain property and another person had a superior right to that property, you must give the property to the beneficiary. If you took the property fraudulently, i.e., you knew you had no right to that property but took it anyway, the beneficiary has the right to sue you for the value of the property plus three times its market value (Probate 13110).

The beneficiary has three years from the date the Affidavit is submitted, or three years from the discovery of the fraud — whichever is the later date (Probate 13110).

GETTING THE CONTENTS OF THE SAFE DEPOSIT BOX

As explained at the end of Chapter 3, if the decedent leased a safe deposit box together with another person, each with full authority to enter the box, the co-lessee of the box can remove all of its contents. If, however, the decedent and another both needed to be present in order to access the box, or if the decedent was the sole lessee of a safe deposit box, the bank will not turn over the contents of the box unless the person making the request gives the bank a document authorizing the transfer (Probate 331).

If the surviving Spouse/RDP obtains an order of NO ADMINISTRATION saying that all of the decedent's property belongs to the Spouse/RDP, the bank will allow the Spouse/RDP to take possession of the contents of the safe deposit box.

If there is a full Probate procedure, the Court will issue Letters to the Personal Representative giving him authority to take possession of all of the assets that belonged to the decedent. With these Letters the Personal Representative can gain access to the decedent's safe deposit box and all of its contents.

If the decedent's gross Estate, including the contents of the safe deposit box, is not greater than $100,000, you can get the contents of the box using the Affidavit just described. If a Personal Representative is appointed, his written permission needs to be attached to the Affidavit.

Probate is not necessary in order to transfer real property located within the state of California, if the decedent owned that property:

⇨ as the owner of a Life Estate - or -

⇨ Jointly With Right of Survivorship - or -

⇨ as Community Property passing to the surviving Spouse/RDP by operation of law - or -

⇨ as Community Property with Rights of Survivorship.

In each of these cases, the property belongs to the surviving owner as of the date of death, however, the decedent's name remains on the deed. Anyone examining title to the property will not know of the death. In California, the Department of Health Services issues the death certificate, but they do not publish the death certificate so it is not part of the public record (Health & Safety 103526).

If Probate is not necessary to transfer other property owned by the decedent, the attorney for the Personal Representative will, within 45 days of the date of death, have a document entitled:

DEATH OF REAL PROPERTY OWNER
CHANGE IN OWNERSHIP STATEMENT

recorded in each county where the decedent owned property. If Probate is not necessary, it is up to the surviving owner to have the Statement filed with the County Recorder or Assessor in the county where the property is located (Rev. & Tax. 480).

You can get a copy of the Change in Ownership Statement from the Clerk in the Department of Registrar-Recorder. However, if you make a mistake in completing the document it might cost considerable time, effort and expense to correct the error.

It is best to have an attorney help you complete and file the document. If you are a joint tenant, he will also prepare and record an AFFIDAVIT OF DEATH OF JOINT TENANT.

If you are a surviving Spouse/RDP and you are inheriting Community Property with No Administration necessary as described earlier you should also record a document with the County Recorder in the county where the property is located, entitled:

SURVIVING SPOUSE'S AFFIDAVIT CONFIRMING
SUCCESSION TO COMMUNITY REAL PROPERTY

TRANSFERRING PROPERTY WORTH $20,000 OR LESS

If the decedent owned real property in his name only, or as a Tenant in Common, then a Probate procedure is necessary unless the property is worth no more than $20,000. California statute allows real property worth $20,000 or less to be transferred to the proper beneficiary by having the beneficiary file an Affidavit in the county where the decedent lived. If the decedent was not a California resident, the Affidavit can be filed in the county where the property is located — once six months from the date of death has passed (Probate 13200).

The Clerk of the Superior Court will give the beneficiary a the form to fill out. He will require the beneficiary to pay a filing fee, and produce several documents, including, the death certificate, receipts showing that the funeral and the costs of the decedent's last illness have been paid, the original Will (if any), the original deed, and an appraisal and inventory showing that the gross value of all of the real property owned by the decedent (not counting non-Probate property) is not worth more than $20,000.

Once the Clerk verifies that six months have passed since the decedent died, and that the information given is correct, he will issue a certified copy of the Affidavit. The certified copy of the Affidavit is then given to the County Recorder who will record the certified copy listing the decedent as the Grantor and the beneficiary of the property as the Grantee. Once the Affidavit is recorded, the beneficiary becomes the owner of the property (Probate 13200, 13202).

Although this is a fine method of transferring real property, it has no practical application. Where in California can you find a parcel of land worth $20,000 or less??

In general, Probate will be necessary if the decedent held real property in his name only or as a Tenants in Common. The attorney for the Personal Representative will prepare and record deed transferring the property to the proper beneficiary. If you are the beneficiary of that property, you should receive the original recorded deed for your records.

| Special Situation | TRANSFERRING OUT OF STATE PROPERTY |

Each state regulates the transfer of real property within that state. Many states do not require that any document be recorded to transfer real property to a surviving Joint Tenant who has a right of survivorship, or to the owner of the remainder interest of a Life Estate. All the surviving owner needs to do is keep a certified copy of the death certificate available to produce at closing when the property is transferred.

Some states allow the death certificate to be recorded in the county where the property is located, so that anyone examining title to the property will know who now owns the property. In other states, (like California) an Affidavit is recorded. If the decedent owned out of state real property in joint tenancy with right of survivor, or if he held a Life Estate interest, you may want to call the recording department in the county where the property is located to find out what documents (if any) need to be recorded. In California, the County Recorder is in charge of recording deeds. In other states, it might be the Clerk of the Circuit Court, or the County Registrar.

Of course, if the decedent owned real property in his own name or as a Tenant In Common, you need to contact an attorney in that state to have the property transferred to the proper beneficiary.

The decedent may have owned a Stock Cooperative apartment that needs to be transferred to a beneficiary. As explained in Chapter 3, a Stock Cooperative ("Co-op") is part of a multi-dwelling complex owned by an Association. Each member of the Association is entitled to exclusive possession of a unit in that complex. The Co-op is generally organized as a corporation, so the interest in the Association is in the form of a share of the corporation. The exclusive possession of the apartment is in the form of a Proprietary Lease (Civil 1351 (m)).

The Co-op is a hybrid involving personal property (a share of the Association) and real property (a proprietary lease to the apartment). To transfer the Co-op, the new owner will need a copy of the Certificate of Incorporation, stock offering prospectus, stock subscription agreement, and the Proprietary Lease.

If Probate is necessary, the attorney for the Personal Representative will see to the transfer of the Co-op. If Probate is not necessary, it is advisable to have an attorney experienced in real property law to be sure that title to the property is properly transferred and taxes on the transfer are paid.

THE FULL PROBATE PROCEDURE

If the decedent died leaving everything to one or two heirs, and an Estate of $100,000 or less and no real property involved, the Affidavit is a simple way to go. If there are two heirs, they can sign a joint Affidavit to get the property. An Affidavit cannot be used to transfer real property whose value is greater than $20,000. And it may not be the best choice if the decedent owed a significant amount of money, because if a full Probate is conducted, creditors must come forward within four months of the granting of Letters to the Personal Representative (Probate 9100). If property is transferred by Affidavit, creditors have a year pursue the matter (Civ. Proc. 366.2).

Of course if the decedent left assets worth more than $100,000, there is no choice in the matter — there needs to be a full Probate Administration. The proceeding can take anywhere from several months to more than a year depending on the size and complexity of the Probate Estate. It is the Personal Representative's job to use the Probate Estate to pay all valid claims and then to distribute what is left to the proper beneficiary, so the first order of business is to appoint a Personal Representative.

APPOINTING THE PERSONAL REPRESENTATIVE

California statute gives an order of priority in the appointment of a Personal Representative. Whoever the decedent named as Personal Representative or Executor of his Will has top priority. If within thirty days of being notified of the death, he fails to ask to be appointed, the Court will consider that he waived (gave up) his right to be Personal Representative (Probate 8001).

If the decedent died without a Will, California statute gives an order of priority for the appointment of a Personal Representative.

1st Spouse/RDP   2nd adult child

3rd adult grandchild

4th other descendants (great-grandchild, etc.)

5th parent   6th brothers and sisters

7th descendants of brother or sister (decedent's nieces, nephews, great-nieces, great-nephews, etc.)

8th grandparent

9th descendants of grandparents (decedent's aunts, uncles, cousins)

10th children of the decedent's predeceased Spouse/RDP

11th other descendants of a predeceased Spouse/RDP

12th other next of kin

13th parents of the decedent's predeceased Spouse/RDP

14th descendants of parents of a predeceased Spouse/RDP

15th someone who was serving as Conservator or Guardian of the decedent, and who has filed an accounting and who is not a Conservator or Guardian for anyone else

16th a public administrator

17th a creditor of the decedent

18th anyone else (Probate 8461).

If the surviving Spouse/RDP was in the process of obtaining a legal separation, or divorce and was living separately, (s)he loses top priority and takes a place after decedent's siblings, i.e., (s)he becomes sixth in priority (Probate 8463).

Usually the family decides among themselves, who they want as a Personal Representative. But if there is disagreement, the choice of Personal Representative will be up to the Court (Probate 8004). The judge will use the above order of priority to make his decision.

The Personal Representative is in charge of settling the Estate. Too often, beneficiaries of the Estate have no idea what is going on. They wait to receive their inheritance, not knowing that they have rights under California law. More importantly, not knowing how to assert those rights.

✧ RIGHT TO BE KEPT INFORMED

Anyone who has an interest in the Estate has the right to be kept informed, provided that person asserts his right by filing a REQUEST FOR SPECIAL NOTICE with the Clerk of the Superior Court. You can file your Request For Special Notice anytime after the Personal Representative is appointed. It is important to do so as soon as possible, so that you can raise any objection you may have in a timely manner.

The Request needs to state your name and address, or the address of your attorney. You should request all of the notices allowed under subdivision (c) of Section 1250 of the Probate code. This includes copies of the following:

▤ Petitions filed in the administration proceeding
▤ Inventories and appraisals of property in the Estate, including any supplemental inventories and appraisals.
▤ Objections to an appraisal
▤ Accounts of a Personal Representative
▤ Reports of status of administration.

File the original Request with the Court and deliver a copy to the Personal Representative or his attorney. You can send it by certified mail or deliver it in person and get a signed receipt. You need to file the receipt together with a *Proof of Service* form provided by the Clerk.

❖ RIGHT TO YOUR OWN ATTORNEY

The attorney who handles the Estate is employed by, and represents, the Personal Representative. If the Estate is sizeable, consider employing your own attorney to check that things are done properly and in a timely manner. Even if the Estate is small, consider consulting with an attorney any time you are concerned about the way the Probate is being conducted.

❖ RIGHT TO OBJECT TO PERSONAL REPRESENTATIVE

Regardless of who has priority to serve, it is the Court who has final say as to who will serve as Personal Representative. The judge can appoint the person with priority, or if the beneficiaries of the Estate object, he can appoint someone who is acceptable to those who have a majority interest in the Estate.

❖ RIGHT TO APPEAR BEFORE THE COURT

Should a problem arise, you have the right to go before the Court on your own, but before doing so, you should consult with an experienced Probate attorney. He can explain the best way for you to present your concerns to the Court. He can tell you what arguments have a good chance of swaying the judge. And he can tell you which arguments have so little probability of success that they are not worth pursuing.

❖ RIGHT TO OBJECT TO THE WILL

The decedent's Will can be admitted into Probate by means of an informal proceeding. You have the right to receive a copy of the Will that is offered for Probate. If you believe the Will is not valid, you can bring your concerns to the attention of the Court. You must do so within 120 days of the Will being accepted into Probate, or within 60 days that you first obtained knowledge of the Will (Probate 8226).

Contesting a Will is one of those issues that requires the assistance of an experienced Probate attorney. The person who offers the Will into Probate is not about to withdraw that Will without a fight. That fight is called litigation — with the validity of the Will being decided at trial.

✧ RIGHT TO DEMAND BOND

It doesn't happen often, but every now and again a Personal Representative will run off with Estate funds. A bond is insurance for the Estate. If Estate monies are stolen then the company that issued the bond will reimburse the Estate for the loss. It is up to the Court to decide whether a bond is necessary, and if so, the value of the bond. When making his decision he will consider:

⇨ whether Estate assets are easily liquidated, i.e., changed to cash

⇨ the identity of the Personal Representative. The Court will not order a bond if the Personal Representative is a trust company (Probate 301).

⇨ whether the Will or the beneficiaries have waived bond.

Most Wills state that no bond shall be required. The reason is two-fold. The Will maker chooses someone he trusts to administer the Estate, so he does not think a bond is necessary. And there are economic reasons. The cost of the bond is paid for by the Estate, and ultimately the amount inherited is reduced by the amount paid for the bond.

In general, the Court will not require bond if the Will or the beneficiaries waive the requirement of a bond. However, if anyone (including a creditor) brings his concerns about the safety of Estate funds, to the attention of the Court. The judge may, for good cause require bond (Probate 8481).

✧ RIGHT TO DEMAND COURT SUPERVISION

The Personal Representative can ask the Court that he be allowed *full authority* to administer the Estate without Court supervision; or he can ask for *limited authority* meaning he can operate independently with the exception of real estate transactions with Estate property (exchanging, selling, giving someone an option to purchase, taking a mortgage on Estate property) (Probate 10401, 10402, 10403). Even with full authority, the Personal Representative will still need to ask the Court to approve certain actions, such as paying fees to himself or his attorney or making a final distribution to the beneficiaries. See statute Probate 10501 for a list of actions that require Court approval.

The Court will not give the Personal Representative authority to act independently unless he notifies all of the beneficiaries that he intends to ask for permission to conduct an **Independent Administration** or unless all of the beneficiaries sign waivers of their right to object (Probate 10451).

Allowing the Personal Representative to act independently may make the Probate move along more quickly because the Personal Representative is relieved of the need to ask the Court for permission before he acts. However, without Court supervision, he may settle claims or sell property without your knowledge or consent. If this is of concern to you, demand Court Supervision.

✧ RIGHT TO KNOW PERSONAL REPRESENTATIVE'S FEES

The Personal Representative is entitled to be compensated for his efforts in settling the Estate. If he is also a beneficiary of the Estate he may decide not to take a commission and just take his inheritance. The reason may be economic. Money inherited from the decedent is not considered to be income to the beneficiary, so there is no federal or state income tax on those funds. However, fees earned by the Personal Representative are taxable as ordinary income. Ask the Personal Representative to tell you, in writing, whether he intends to charge a fee, and if so, how much.

There are statutory guidelines for what is "reasonable" compensation for the Personal Representative. If he elects to be paid, his compensation will be based on the value of the Estate as valued on the inventory, plus or minus gains or losses on the sale of Estate property, plus receipts.

4% on the first $100,000 ($4,000)
3% on the next $100,000 ($3,000)
2% on the next $800,000 ($16,000)
1% on the next $9,000,000 ($90,000)
one half of 1% on the next $15,000,000 ($75,000)

The Court will determine a reasonable compensation for values over $25,000,000 (Probate 10800).

A beneficiary of the Estate cannot agree to having the Personal Representative receive more compensation than allowed under California law. However, the Court can increase the amount due to the Personal Representative for any extraordinary service performed in settling the Estate such as pursuing a lawsuit on behalf of the Estate (Probate 10801, 10803).

✧ RIGHT TO KNOW ATTORNEY'S FEES

It is the Personal Representative's job to use the Probate Estate to pay all valid claims and then distribute what is left to the proper beneficiary. Debts are paid from the decedent's Estate and not from the Personal Representative's pocket; but if he makes a mistake, he may be responsible to pay for it. For example, if the Personal Representative sells property for less than its market value, he may be personally liable to those who suffered a loss because of his negligence or misconduct (Probate 10380).

The Personal Representative needs to employ an attorney to guide him through the Probate procedure so that things will be done properly and at no personal cost to the Representative. It is proper to have the attorney paid with Estate funds. Under California law, the attorney is entitled to the same fee schedule as is that of the Personal Representative as stated on the prior page (Probate 10810).

However, there is no law saying that he cannot accept less. Notice that under California law, a "reasonable" attorney fee for an Estate of $200,000 is $7,000. It may be that the decedent's Estate has easily liquidated assets, only one or two beneficiaries, and no creditor problems. In such case, the work in settling the Estate should be minimal and it is proper to "shop around" to find an attorney who will agree to less than the statutory amount.

Although the Personal Representative can negotiate a lower attorney fee, he may not agree to pay more than that allowed by law (Probate 10813). However, if there is some difficulty in settling the Estate, the attorney can ask the Court to award him additional compensation for extraordinary services, such as a Will contest, or a dispute with a creditor (Probate 10811).

✧ RIGHT TO COPY OF INVENTORY

The Personal Representative must prepare an inventory of all of the assets of the Probate Estate within four months of his appointment and file it with the Court. The Personal Representative is required to send a copy of the inventory to any interested party who filed a Request For Special Notice with the Court (Probate 1250, 8800). The value of the inventory is used to determine the Representative's fees and to determine how much taxes need to be paid. It is important that you receive a copy of the inventory, and that you are satisfied with the value assigned to each item.

✧ RIGHT TO AN APPRAISAL

A Probate Referee has the job of making appraisals for the Probate Court. To get the job, he must pass a qualifying examination and be appointed by the Controller of the state of California (Probate 400, 402). The Probate Referee will appraise the decedent's property, however, in some cases no formal appraisal is necessary because the Estate consists of bank accounts and securities whose value is easily determined by the Personal Representative (Probate 8901). The Personal Representative has the right to petition (ask) the Court to waive a formal appraisal. The law requires that each beneficiary of the Will be served with petition and a copy of the proposed inventory (Probate 8903). If you are concerned about the proposed evaluation, you need to ask for a formal appraisal.

Once an appraisal is made you have the right to object if you feel an item was given too high, or too low a value. A hearing will be set on the matter. It is prudent to consult with an attorney before raising any objection because the Court can charge you for attorney's fees if he finds that your challenge was without reasonable cause (Probate 8906).

✧ RIGHT TO PERSONAL PROPERTY

Sometimes it costs more to store personal property than it is worth. The Personal Representative has the right to throw it away or give it away, but before doing so, he must tell you what he is going to do at least five days before he does it. If he sends you notice by mail, he must deposit the letter at least ten days before the action. You can ask that he give you the property rather than abandon it. If he refuses, you will need to move quickly to ask the Court to stop him from taking such action (Probate 9782).

✧ RIGHT TO AN ACCOUNTING

Before closing the Estate the Personal Representative must file an accounting of how Estate funds were spent beginning with the value of the inventory and ending with the amount on hand. He will file a petition for an Order of Final Distribution which will state how he intends to distribute whatever is left. All beneficiaries are entitled to a copy of the accounting and Petition For Final Distribution, regardless of whether they filed Request For Special Notice with the Court (Probate 10831).

If the Estate has significant assets, you may want your own accountant to look over the accounting. If there are any problems that your accountant can not resolve with the Personal Representative, you can object to the accounting and raise these issues at a hearing before the Court (Probate 11001).

You may be asked to sign a waiver of your right to an accounting, but keep in mind that the accounting is for your benefit. There are few situations that justify you giving up your right to know how Estate monies were spent.

✧ RIGHT TO HAVE THE ESTATE CLOSED WITHOUT DELAY

How long it takes to complete the Probate proceeding depends on the size and complexity of the matter. Creditors have four months to file a claim from the day Letters were issued to the Personal Representative or 60 days after the creditor was given Notice of Administration — whichever is the later (Probate 9100). The Court will not allow the Estate to be closed until all of the creditors have had an opportunity to come forward and present their claims. If a federal Estate Tax return has been filed, it will probably take a year or more to obtain a tax release.

The Personal Representative should file a Petition for an *Order Of Final Distribution* within one year from the day the he received his Letters — or within 18 months if an Estate Tax return was filed (Probate 12200). If there is some problem with closing the Estate, such as a conflict over the validity of the Will, the Personal Representative should make a *Report of Status of Administration* within these time periods. If you have not received either of these documents within the given time periods, you have the right to ask the Court to order the Personal Representative to give a final accounting and plan of distribution (Probate 10950).

✧ RIGHT TO RECEIVE A DEBT FREE INHERITANCE

Once a beneficiary finally receives his inheritance, about the last thing he wants to hear is that there is some unfinished business, or worse yet that monies need to be paid from the inheritance he received. But that is just what could happen if the Personal Representative distributes the money before all the creditors are paid. An unpaid creditor could sue the beneficiary any time within one year from the date of death (Civ. Proc. 366.2)

Ask the Personal Representative whether he gave written notice to all known creditors as required by Probate statute (Probate 9050). And if not, whether he is aware of any outstanding debts. Taxes are another concern. If the Personal Representative fails to file a return, or if he under reports a tax obligation, you could be called on to pay taxes out of the proceeds that you receive. To avoid the problem ask to see a copy of all of the tax returns that were filed, and then verify that any monies that were due have been paid.

IT'S YOUR RIGHT - DON'T BE INTIMIDATED

You may feel uncomfortable being assertive with a friend or family member who is Personal Representative. Don't be. It's your money and your right to be informed. Be especially firm if the Personal Representative waves you off with "You've known me for years. Surely you trust me." People who are trustworthy, don't ask to be trusted. They do what is right. The very fact that the Personal Representative is resisting, is a red flag. In such situation, you can explain that it is not a matter of trust, but a matter of your legal rights.

At the same time, keep things in perspective. Your relationship with the Personal Representative may be more important to you than the money you inherit. The job of settling an Estate can be complex and demanding. If the Personal Representative is getting the job done, let him know you appreciate his efforts.

Once the Probate proceeding is over, you will be left with many documents and wonder which you need to keep:

COURT DOCUMENTS

You should keep a copy of the inventory to establish the value of property that you inherit. That value becomes your basis for any Capital Gains Tax that you may need to pay in the future. Other than the inventory, there is no reason to keep any Court document, provided you are satisfied with the way things were done and do not intend to take action against the Personal Representative, or his attorney. The Clerk of the Probate Court keeps the Probate file on record, so if for some reason you later need a copy of a Probate document, you can get it from the Clerk.

PERSONAL RECORDS

The surviving Spouse/RDP, or if no Spouse/RDP, his next of kin should keep the decedent's personal papers (birth certificate, death certificate, marriage certificate, naturalization papers, military records, religious documents, etc.). They may be needed in order to apply for government, or other, benefits. The next of kin may want to keep the decedent's medical records in the event that a family member needs to investigate a genetic disorder.

TAX RECORDS

The IRS has up to three years to collect additional taxes, and you have up to seven years to claim a loss from a worthless security, so you should keep the decedent's tax file for seven years from the date of filing the return. You can learn more about which records to keep from the IRS publication 552. You can get the publication by calling the IRS at (800) 829-3676 or you can download it from their Website: http://www.irs.gov

THE CHECK LIST

We discussed many things that need to be done when some-one dies in the state of California. The next page contains a check list that you may find helpful.

You can check those items that you need to do, and then cross them off the list once they are done. We made the list as comprehensive as possible, so many items may not apply in your case. In such case, you can cross them off the list or mark them *N/A* (not applicable).

Things To Do

FUNERAL ARRANGEMENTS TO BE MADE
☐ AUTOPSY ☐ ANATOMICAL GIFT
☐ DISPOSITION OF BODY OR ASHES

DEATH CERTIFICATE
GIVE COPY TO: _____

_____

_____

NOTICE OF DEATH
PEOPLE TO BE NOTIFIED _____

_____

COMPANIES TO NOTIFY
☐ CREDIT CARD COMPANIES
☐ TELEPHONE COMPANY
    ☐ LOCAL CARRIER ☐ LONG DISTANCE ☐ CELLULAR
☐ NEWSPAPER (OBITUARY PRINTED)
☐ NEWSPAPER DELIVERY CANCELLED ☐ deposit refund
☐ SOCIAL SECURITY
☐ POWER & LIGHT ☐ deposit refund
☐ POST OFFICE
☐ OTHER UTILITIES (GAS, WATER) ☐ deposit refund
☐ PENSION PLAN ☐ ANNUITY
☐ HEALTH INSURANCE COMPANY
☐ LIFE INSURANCE COMPANY
☐ HOME INSURANCE COMPANY
☐ MOTOR VEHICLE INSURANCE COMPANY
☐ CONDOMINIUM OR HOMEOWNER ASSOCIATION

NOTICE AND CANCEL
☐ CANCEL INTERNET SERVER
☐ CANCEL TELEVISION CABLE/SATELLITE COMPANY
☐ CANCEL SERVICE CONTRACT ☐ deposit refund
☐ CANCEL DRIVER'S LICENSE, OR PHOTO ID
☐ CANCEL VOTER REGISTRATION

Things To Do

REMOVE DECEDENT AS BENEFICIARY OF YOUR:

☐ WILL ☐ INSURANCE POLICY ☐ PENSION PLAN
☐ BANK OR IRA ACCOUNT ☐ SECURITIES

DEBTS

PAY DECEDENT'S DEBTS (AMOUNT & CREDITOR)

_____

COLLECT MONIES OWED TO DECEDENT (AMOUNT & DEBTOR)

_____

TAXES

☐ FILE FINAL FEDERAL INCOME TAX RETURN
☐ FILE FINAL STATE INCOME TAX RETURN
☐ RECEIVE INCOME TAX REFUND
☐ FILE ESTATE TAX RETURN

PROPERTY TO BE TRANSFERRED

☐ PERSONAL EFFECTS
☐ MOTOR VEHICLE
☐ BANK ACCOUNT
☐ CREDIT UNION ACCOUNT
☐ IRA ACCOUNT
☐ SECURITIES
☐ BROKERAGE ACCOUNT
☐ INSURANCE PROCEEDS
☐ HOMESTEAD
☐ TIME SHARE
☐ OTHER REAL PROPERTY
☐ CONTENTS OF SAFE DEPOSIT BOX

OTHER THINGS TO DO

_____
_____
_____

Everyman's Estate Plan 7

The first six chapters of this book describe how to wind up the affairs of the decedent. As you read those chapters, you learned about the kinds of problems that can occur when settling the decedent's Estate. It is relatively simple for you to set up an Estate Plan so that your family members are not burdened with similar problems. An *Estate Plan* is the arranging of your finances for maximum control and protection during your lifetime, and at the same time ensuring that your property will be transferred quickly and at little cost to your heirs.

If you think that only wealthy people need to prepare an Estate Plan, you are mistaken. Each year, heirs of relatively modest Estates, spend thousands of dollars to settle an Estate. A bit of planning could have eliminated most, if not all, of the expense and hassle suffered by those families.

The suggestions in this chapter are designed to assist the average person in preparing a practical and inexpensive Estate Plan, so we named this chapter EVERYMAN'S ESTATE PLAN.

Once you create your own Estate Plan, you can be assured that your family will not be left with more problems than happy memories of you.

AVOIDING PROBATE

After reading the last Chapter, many will come to the conclusion that Probate is a good thing to avoid. Those who have $100,000 or less in personal property and no real property may not be concerned with avoiding Probate because your beneficiaries can get possession of that property with little effort or expense.

But if you own personal property in excess of $100,000 or real property in excess of $20,000, in your name only, a full Probate will be necessary with all of its inherent delays and expenses. Notice that the operative phrase in the last sentence is *in your name only*. Whether a Probate procedure is necessary depends on how your property is titled (owned). It makes no difference whether you do or do not have a Will. If you own personal property in excess of $100,000 or real property in excess of $20,000, and that property is titled in your name only, with no provision for a non-Probate transfer, your beneficiaries will need to go through Probate in order to get possession of that property.

As explained in Chapter 5, there are many ways to title real property so that it passes automatically without the need for Probate. For example, if you own real property Jointly With Rights of Survivorship, upon your death, the survivors will own the property without the need to go through Probate. Similarly if you own a Life Estate, upon your death, the property passes directly to the owner of the remainder interest in the property.

In this Chapter, we examine ways to title your personal property (bank accounts, securities, etc.) so that it passes to your beneficiaries without the need for Probate.

OWNERSHIP OF BANK ACCOUNTS

You can arrange to have all of your bank accounts set up so that should you die, the money goes directly to a beneficiary. For example, suppose all you own is a bank account and you want whatever you have in the account to go to your son and daughter when you die. You might think that a simple solution is to put each child's name on the account as Joint Tenants, but first consider the problems associated with a joint account.

⊠ POTENTIAL LIABILITY

If you hold a bank account jointly with your adult child and that child is sued or gets a divorce, the child may need to disclose his ownership of the joint account. In such a case, you may find yourself spending money to prove that the account was established for your convenience only and that all of the money in that account really belongs to you.

⊠ OVERREACHING

If you set up a joint account with your child so that the child has authority to withdraw funds from the account, monies could be withdrawn without your knowledge or consent.

If you have a joint account with two of your children, there is the problem of what happens to the funds after your death. Unless your agreement with the bank states differently, should you die, each child is entitled to their share of the account plus half of your net contribution to the account (Probate 5302). But as a practical matter, each joint owner has free access to the bank account. After your death it could become a race to the bank. If one child withdraws all of the money that will, at the very least, cause hard feelings between them.

THE BENEFICIARY ACCOUNT

Holding a bank account jointly with a family member eliminates the need for Probate, but at the cost of control of the funds. One way to avoid Probate of the account yet retain full control during your lifetime, is to name one or more persons to be the beneficiary of the account (Probate 5504). There are two forms of **Beneficiary Account**. You can open a **Totten Trust Account** holding the funds in trust for one or more beneficiaries that you name or you can have a contract with the bank that directs the bank to **Pay On Death** ("POD") all of the money in the account to one or more beneficiaries that you name.

The Totten Trust Account is different from an account that is opened by the Trustee under a written Trust Agreement. The Account is regulated only by your agreement with the bank that upon your death the money on deposit is inherited by the beneficiary that you name (Probate 80). We will discuss a bank account opened by a Trustee under a Trust Agreement later in this chapter.

The contract you sign with the bank gives instructions that the bank will follow should you die while the account is open. If you open a Totten Trust or Pay On Death account, unless the contract with your bank states differently, under California law:

⇨   The beneficiary has no right to your account during your lifetime. You are free to change beneficiaries without asking his permission to do so.

⇨   If you name two or more beneficiaries, the funds are divided equally between them upon your death. Unless your agreement with the bank states otherwise, if one of your beneficiary dies, the surviving beneficiary will inherit the account. (Probate 5301, 5302).

TRANSFER ON DEATH SECURITIES

The California law for securities is much the same as the statutes for bank accounts. You can arrange to have a security (a stock, bond or brokerage account) transferred to a beneficiary upon your death. You can instruct the holder of the security to Pay On Death or **Transfer On Death** ("TOD") to a named beneficiary (Probate 5505). If the beneficiary of the security dies before you, the security will become part of your Estate. However, you can direct that if the beneficiary dies first, his descendants inherit the security. For example, a security account can be titled as: Alice Lee, Henry Lee, JT TEN TOD Wayne Lee LDPS, which is short-hand for:

> Alice Lee and Henry Lee are the joint owners of the securities account. Once both are deceased, transfer the securities to Wayne Lee. If Wayne dies before his parents, give the securities to Wayne's lineal descendants, per stirpes.

This is much the same as the POD account. Wayne has no right to the securities until both his parents die. They are free to close the account or to change beneficiaries, without permission from Wayne (Probate 5506, 5507, 5510).

If your Estate consists only of bank accounts and/or securities, and you want all of your property to go to one or two beneficiaries without the need for Probate, but with maximum control and protection of your funds during your lifetime, holding your property in any of these beneficiary forms: *Totten Trust*
Pay On Death
Transfer On Death
should accomplish your goal.

GIFT TO A MINOR CHILD

At the beginning of this chapter, we identified two problems with a joint account: potential liability if the joint owner is sued and overreaching by the joint owner. If you wish to make a gift to a minor child, that presents still another problem. The POD and TOD account avoid the problem of potential liability and overreaching, but if the beneficiary of such account is a minor, there is the problem of the child having access to a large sum of money. Under California law, if the amount in the account is under $10,000 the financial institution can transfer the funds to a trust company or to an adult member of the minor's family. If the amount exceeds that amount the financial institution will not transfer the funds without authorization from the Probate Court (Probate 3907). The Court may decide to appoint a Guardian to care for the child's property until he is 18.

You may think it best that the child inherits more than $10,000 so that a Court will see to it that the monies are held safely till the child is an adult. But that only presents a new set of problems. It takes time, effort and money to set up a guardianship. If you leave the child a significant amount of money, the Guardian has the right to be paid to manage those funds. It could happen that the cost of maintaining the guardianship significantly reduces the amount of money inherited by the child.

There are ways to avoid the problem of having a Guardian appointed to care for property inherited by a child, and yet ensuring that the property is protected. One such method is the **CALIFORNIA UNIFORM TRANSFERS TO MINORS ACT.**

THE UNIFORM TRANSFERS TO MINORS ACT

The *California Uniform Transfers to Minors Act* is designed to protect gifts made to a minor by appointing someone to be the *Custodian* of a gift until the child is an adult. The Custodian can be a trusted friend or relative, or you can name a bank or other financial institution to serve as Custodian. It is appropriate to use the Uniform Transfers To Minors Act if you want to make the child a beneficiary of your Will or of a life insurance policy, or even of a bank account. For example, you can name the bank as Custodian of the bank account in the event that you die before the child is an adult.

> RUSSELL JONES POD FRIENDLY BANK as Custodian
> For RUSSELL JONES, JR. under the California Uniform
> Transfers to Minors Act (Probate 3909).

During your lifetime you can add to the account or close it or change beneficiaries, or even appoint someone else to serve as Custodian of the property (Probate 3903).

LIFETIME GIFTS

You can use the Uniform Transfers to Minors Act to make a gift during your lifetime of some item such as a shares in a corporation or a limited partnership interest. You can nominate yourself as Custodian of the gift, or you can name another person to serve as Custodian. Once the lifetime gift is made it becomes irrevocable, so this method is not appropriate unless you are sure that you want the child to have the gift once (s)he is 18 (Probate 3904, 3909).

In general, the Custodian must distribute the gift when the child reaches 18; however, gifts made by Will can be held by the Custodian until the child is 26, and a lifetime gift can be held up to the age of 25. If you do not give written direction as to the age of distribution, the Custodian will distribute the gift on or before his 18th birthday (Probate 3920, 3920.5).

The Custodian needs to invest and manage the property in a responsible, prudent manner. He must keep records of all transactions made with custodial property; and make those records available for inspection by the child's parent, or other interested person, or the child, if he is 14 or older. If those records are not to their satisfaction, they can petition (ask) the Probate Court to require the Custodian to give an accounting (Probate 3912, 3919).

The Custodian can use as much of the gift as he thinks advisable for the benefit of the child. He can pay monies directly to the child, or use the funds for the child's benefit. In making the distribution he is not obliged to take into account that someone else has a duty to support the child — even if the Custodian is the child's parent and it is his responsibility to support the child (Probate 3914). If the Custodian wants to keep the funds invested, any interested person, or the child once he is 14, can ask the Court to order the Custodian to part with some or all of the money for the benefit of the child. The judge will decide what is in the child's best interest and then rule on the matter.

The Custodian is entitled to be paid for his effort each year (Probate 3915). If the gift is sizeable, the Custodian's fee can be sizeable. Before appointing a person or a financial institution as Custodian, it is best to come to a written agreement about what will be charged to manage the custodial property.

A gift made under the California Uniform Transfers to Minors Act is limited to one minor only (Probate 3910). If you want to give a single gift, such as a gift of real property to two or more children or if you want more flexibility about when the minor is to receive the gift, then a Trust may be the better way to go. We discuss Trusts later in this chapter.

THE GIFT OF REAL PROPERTY

As explained in Chapter 5, if you own real property together with another, then who owns the property upon your death depends on how the Grantee is identified on the face of the deed. If you compare the Grantee clause of the deed to the examples given in Chapter 5 you can determine who will inherit the property when you die. If you are not satisfied with the way the property will be inherited, you need to consult with an attorney to change the deed so that it will conform to your wishes.

If you own the property in your name only or as a Tenant In Common, when you die, there will need to be a Probate proceeding to determine the proper beneficiary of that land. If your main objective is to avoid Probate, you can have an attorney change the deed so that upon your death, the property will go to your beneficiary without the need for Probate. As with bank and securities accounts there are different ways to do so, each with its own advantages and disadvantages.

JOINT OWNERSHIP

If you hold property in your name only, and wish to avoid Probate, you can have your deed changed so that you and a beneficiary are joint owners with rights of survivorship. If you do so, should either of you die, the other will own the property 100%. That avoids Probate, but by making that person joint owner, you are, in effect, making a gift of half of the property during your lifetime. You will not be able to sell that property without the beneficiary's permission. And if the beneficiary gives permission and the property is sold, the beneficiary will have the legal right to half of the proceeds of the sale.

And you may be creating a Capital Gains Tax problem as well. As explained on page 45, you can arrange to sell your home without paying a Capital Gains Tax, but if you make someone joint owner of your home who does not live with you, a Capital Gains Tax may need to be paid on the joint owner's share of the proceeds should you decide to sell the property.

 ## GIFT OF HOMESTEAD

Some elderly parents worry that they may need nursing care at some time in the future and lose all of their life savings to pay for that care. The parent may decide that the best way to avoid Probate and protect the homestead from loss is to transfer the homestead to their child with the understanding that the parent will continue to live there until he/she dies. But this is just trading risks.

⊠   RISK OF LOSS

Property transferred to your child could be lost if the child runs into serious financial difficulties or is sued. This is especially a risk if your child is a professional (doctor, nurse, accountant, financial planner, attorney, etc.). If your child is (or gets) married, this complicates matters even more. Should the child divorce, the property may need to be included as part of the settlement agreement. This may be to your child's detriment, because the child may need to share the value of the property with his/her former spouse. If you do not transfer the property, it cannot become part of the marital equation.

⊠ LOSS OF HOMESTEAD CREDITOR PROTECTION

As explained in Chapter 4, the homestead of a California resident is protected against creditors. The amount of protection varies from $50,000 up to $150,000 depending on the circumstances of the owner of the property (Civ. Proc. 704.730). With the exception of mechanic's liens, property taxes and mortgages on your homestead, none of your creditors can force the sale of your property unless you owe them more than the amount allowed under California statute (Civ. Proc. 704.995). If you simply transfer your homestead to a child, you lose this creditor protection.

If you are married or a Domestic Partner, it is a double loss of creditor protection. Not only do you lose protection for yourself, you lose it for your Spouse/RDP as well. If you transfer your homestead to your child and he does not occupy that property as his homestead, there is no homestead creditor protection whatsoever. The child's creditors can force the sale of the property (that's your home) for relatively small amounts of unpaid debts.

⊠ POSSIBLE GIFT TAX

If the value of the transfer is worth more than the Annual Gift Tax Exclusion ($12,000 as of 2007) you need to file a Gift Tax return. For most of us, this is not a problem because no Gift Tax need be paid unless the equity in your home (fair market value less mortgages on the property) plus the value of all gifts in excess of the Annual Gift Tax Exclusion that you gave over your lifetime, exceed $1,000,000 (see Chapter 2). But if your Estate is in that tax bracket, you need to be aware that you are "using up" your lifetime Gift Tax Exclusion.

⊠   POSSIBLE CAPITAL GAINS TAX

Although certain members of Congress has expressed a desire to phase out the Estate Tax, there is no discussion to do away with the Capital Gains Tax. If you gift the property to the child during your lifetime, when he sells the property he will pay a Capital Gains Tax on the increase in value from the price you paid for your home to the selling price at the time your child sells the property.

If you do not make the gift during your lifetime, the child will inherit the property with a step-up in basis, i.e., he will inherit the property at its market value as of your date of death. Under today's tax structure and continuing through 2009, that step-up in basis is unlimited. If your child sells the property shortly after he inherits it, he will pay no Capital Gains Tax, regardless of how large the step-up in basis.

In 2010, there will be a limit on the amount that can be inherited free of the Capital Gains Tax; but as explained on page 44, that limit is quite high, so for most of us this is not a concern.

⊠   POSSIBLE INCOME TAX ISSUES

Should you give your home to your child and continue to live there, the IRS will expect you to pay rent to your children. If not, the IRS may consider the fair rental value to be a taxable gift from your child to you subject to the Annual Gift Tax Exclusion. Worse yet, the IRS may consider the "rent" to be taxable income to your child.

☒ LOSS OF HOMEOWNERS' PROPERTY TAX EXEMPTION

As explained on page 46, each home owner is entitled to a Homeowners' Property Tax Exemption for California property occupied as his principal residence. In addition, there are special tax exemptions for a disabled Veteran and his surviving Spouse/RDP (Rev. & Tax 205.5, 218). If you put the deed in the beneficiary's name and that property is your homestead, you will lose your Homeowners' Property Tax Exemption. It could cost more money in taxes to continue to live in your own home.

It may be possible to keep your Homeowners' Property Tax Exemption by transferring the property to a beneficiary and keeping a Life Estate for yourself or owning the property jointly with the beneficiary. But there are problems associated with the transfer:

JOINT OWNERSHIP/LIFE ESTATE NOT A COMPLETE SOLUTION

⊳ You cannot sell the property during your lifetime without the beneficiary agreeing to the sale.

⊳ If you sell the property, the beneficiary is entitled to some portion of the proceeds of the sale.

⊳ If you or your beneficiary become incapacitated, the property cannot be sold unless a Conservator is appointed by the Court and the judge approves the sale.

Before you decide to transfer your homestead to a beneficiary, call your local County Assessor and ask if there will be any tax consequence as a result of the transfer.

⊠   POSSIBLE LOSS OF GOVERNMENT BENEFITS

If you transfer property, depending upon the value of the transfer, you could be disqualified from receiving Medi-Cal or Supplemental Security Income ("SSI") benefits for a substantial period of time. Under the Deficit Reduction Act that was signed into law on February 8, 2006, whoever applies for Medicaid, must disclose if, within five years of his application, he transferred property for less than the fair market value (i.e., he gifted property).

The DEPARTMENT OF HEALTH SERVICES is the agency that administers the Medi-Cal program in the state of California. If you apply for Medi-Cal within five years of the transfer of your home, they will compute a disqualification period depending on the value of the transfer. The disqualification period begins on the day you apply for Medi-Cal. This can present a serious problem because you wouldn't be applying unless you exhausted your assets and needed Medi-Cal to cover your medical expenses. Unless the equity in your home exceeds $500,000 ($750,000 in some states) owning a home will not disqualify you from applying for Medi-Cal, but making a gift or your home might.

Under current state and federal law, there are many ways to protect your homestead and still qualify for government benefits. The authors have written a book entitled *A Will Is Not Enough In California*. It contains a discussion of different methods you can use to protect your assets, while ensuring that you receive the medical assistance you may need in your later years.

Before making any transfer of real property, it is important to consult with and Elder Law attorney. You may also want to confer with a certified financial planner and/or accountant, to examine other aspects related to the transfer.

THE PROBLEM OF OUT OF STATE PROPERTY

As explained in Chapter 6, each state is in charge of the way property located in that state is transferred. If you own property in another state (or country), you need to consult with an attorney in that state (or country) to determine how that property will be transferred to your beneficiaries should you die.

If you own property in another state in your name only, or as a Tenant In Common, or if you hold property with your spouse in a Community Property state, a Probate proceeding may need to be held in that state. If it is necessary to have a Probate in California, a second (ancillary) Probate may need to be held in the state where the property is located. This could have the effect of doubling the cost of Probate.

One way to avoid Probate is to title your property so that it is transferred to your beneficiary upon your death, such as Joint Tenants With Right of Survivorship. Another way to avoid the need for Probate, in this or any other state, is to set up a Trust and place your property into your Trust.

CREATING A TRUST

A full Probate procedure may be necessary if you hold property in your name only or as a Tenant In Common. We explored different ways to re-title property to avoid Probate, but these methods have trade-offs that may be unacceptable to you. One way to avoid many of these potential problems is to set up a **Revocable Living Trust** (also known as an *Inter Vivos Trust*).

A Revocable Living Trust is designed to care for your property during your lifetime, and then to distribute your property once you die — without the need for Probate. You may have been encouraged to set up a Trust by your financial planner, attorney, or accountant. Even people of modest means are being encouraged to use a Trust as the basis of their Estate Plan. But Trusts have their pros and cons. Before getting into that, let's first discuss what a Trust is and how it works.

SETTING UP A TRUST

To create a Trust, a person has his attorney prepare a Trust document (a *Trust Agreement*) according to the client's needs and desires. The Agreement is between the person who creates and funds the Trust (the **Settlor** or *Grantor*) and the **Trustee** (manager) of property placed in the Trust. The Settlor usually appoints himself as Trustee so that he is in total control of property he places into the Trust. This means that he signs the Trust Agreement as the Settlor and also as the Trustee who promises to manage the property according to the terms of the Trust Agreement. The Trust document also names a **Successor Trustee** who will take over the management of the Trust property should the Trustee resign, become disabled, or die. We will refer to the Revocable Living Trust as the "Living Trust" or just the "Trust" and the person who creates the Trust as the "Settlor."

Once the Trust Agreement is properly signed, the Settlor transfers property into the Trust. He does this by changing title from his individual name to his name as Trustee. For example, if Elaine Richards sets up a Trust naming herself as Trustee, and she wishes to place her bank account into the Trust, all she need do is instruct the bank to change the name on the account from Elaine Richards to:

ELAINE RICHARDS, TRUSTEE OF THE ELAINE RICHARDS REVOCABLE TRUST AGREEMENT DATED JULY 12, 2005.

When the change is made, all the money in the account becomes Trust property. Elaine (wearing her Trustee hat) has total control of the account, taking money out, and putting money in, as she sees fit. Similarly, if she wants to put real property into the Trust, she can have her attorney prepare a new deed with the owner identified as ELAINE RICHARDS, TRUSTEE. See page 134 for an example of real property placed into a Trust.

During her lifetime, Elaine is free to *amend* (change the terms) her Trust or even terminate (revoke) the Trust altogether and have the Trust property placed back into her own name. If she does not revoke her Trust during her lifetime, once she dies the Trust becomes irrevocable, and her Successor Trustee must follow the terms of the Trust Agreement as written. If the Trust says to give the Trust property to certain beneficiaries, the Successor Trustee will do so, and without the need for Probate. If the Trust directs the Successor Trustee to hold property in Trust and use the money to take care of a member of Elaine's family, in the manner described in the Trust Agreement, the Successor Trustee will do so.

Setting up a Trust has many good features.

☆☆ AVOID PROBATE

In California, Probate can be time consuming and very expensive. Both the Personal Representative and his attorney are entitled to payment for their services. These fees can be significant. It may be necessary to employ accountants and appraisers, and real estate brokers to sell property as well. If you have property in two states, then two Probate procedures may be necessary (one in each state) and that could be costly in time, effort and money. If the Trust is properly drafted and your property placed into the Trust, you should be able to avoid Probate altogether.

☆ FEDERAL ESTATE TAX SAVINGS

Many people think that the federal Estate Tax will be phased out so that by 2010, no Estate Taxes will be due regardless of the size of an Estate. But under current law in 2011, the Estate Tax is scheduled to be reinstated and those who own property worth more than $1,000,000 will once again be subject to a sizeable Estate Tax. A couple with an Estate in excess of a million dollars can reduce the risk of an Estate Tax by setting up a Trust, so that each partner can take advantage of his own Estate Tax Exclusion.

For example, if a couple's assets total two million dollars, they can set up a Trust that separates the money into two Trusts when one partner dies. The Trust can be arranged so that the surviving spouse is free to use the income from both Trusts. Once both partners are deceased, the beneficiaries of their respective Trusts will inherit the funds, hopefully with no Estate Tax due. If the couple does not set up a Trust and they continue to hold all of their property jointly, the last to die will own the two million dollars with only one Estate Tax Exclusion available. This means one million dollars will be subject to Estate Taxes.

☆ CARE FOR FAMILY MEMBER:

You can make provision in your Trust to care for a minor child or family member after you die. If your beneficiary is a minor, you can direct your Successor Trustee to distribute the child's inheritance at different times. For example, you can direct your Successor Trustee to give the beneficiary a certain amount of money when he is 18, then 21, then 25, then 30, etc.

If your intended beneficiary has trouble managing his finances you can set up a *Spendthrift Trust*. You can direct your Successor Trustee to spend Trust funds for your beneficiary's health care, education, and living expenses, and nothing more (Probate 15300). Although your Trustee may be able to protect the beneficiary from his own improvidence, the Trust is not creditor proof. A creditor can ask a Court to order the Trustee to pay a judgment against the beneficiary from funds due to him (Probate 15307). And the Trust funds are not protected from alimony and support payments. If the beneficiary of a Spendthrift Trust owes alimony and/or child support, a judge may order the Trustee to make payment out of all or part of future payments to the beneficiary (Probate 15305).

NO CREDITOR PROTECTION FOR SETTLOR

Because property held in your Revocable Living Trust is freely accessible to you, it is likewise accessible to your creditors both before and after your death. If you die owing money, your creditors can have a Personal Representative appointed to locate funds to pay those debts. The Personal Representative can require that your Trust property be used to pay monies you owe (Probate 15304, Civ. Proc. 695.030).

☆ PRIVACY

Your Living Trust is a private document. No one but your Successor Trustee and your beneficiaries need ever read it. If you leave property in a Will and there is a Probate procedure, the Will must be filed with the court, where it becomes a public document. Anyone can go to the courthouse, read your Will and see who you did (or did not) provide for in your Will. Records in the Probate Court (inventories, creditor's claims, etc.) are open to public scrutiny. In some states, Court records are now available on the Internet!

LEASE SAFE DEPOSIT BOX AS TRUSTEE

One of the benefits of having a Living Trust is that you can lease the safe deposit box in your name as Trustee. When you lease the safe deposit box you can have an agreement with the bank that they are to allow your Successor Trustee free access to the safe deposit box in the event of your incapacity or death.

This protects your privacy. As explained at the end of Chapter 3, if you lease a safe deposit box in your name only, access to the box is restricted upon your death. No one can take possession of the contents of your box without a Court order, but whoever finds the key to your safe deposit box can ask the bank to be allowed to examine the contents of the box to see if your Will is there. Under California law, the bank can allow such inspection, provided a bank officer or employee is present to take an inventory of the contents of the box (Probate 331).

By leasing a safe deposit box as Trustee, only you and your Successor Trustee need ever know of the contents of the box.

☆☆ AVOID APPOINTMENT OF A CONSERVATOR

Once you have a Trust you do not need to worry about who will take care of property you place in the Trust. Should you become disabled or too aged to handle your finances your Successor Trustee will take over the care of the Trust. If you do not make provision for the care of your property, it may be necessary for a Court to appoint a Conservator of your property. Conservatorship is a good thing to avoid, not only because of the cost of the procedure, but also to avoid the embarrassment of a Court coming to the conclusion that you are not competent to manage your own finances.

Before appointing a Conservator, the Court will have a hearing to determine whether you are competent to manage your property. You are entitled to your own attorney at the hearing. If you do not have one the Court can appoint an attorney for you (Probate 1470). If the judge determines that you do not have the capacity to handle your finances, he will appoint a Conservator of your property (Probate 1800.3). He may require a bond for the protection of your property (Probate 2320).

Once appointed, the Conservator will take possession of your property and within 90 days file an inventory with the Court (Probate 2610). The Conservator will manage your property and each year account to the Court for money spent (Probate 2620). He may need to employ an accountant to assist with these reports. The Conservator needs to employ an attorney to establish the conservator-ship and see that it is properly administered. The Conservator, and his attorney, are entitle to be paid for their efforts on you behalf (Probate 2640). Court filing fees, the cost of a bond, accounting fees, Conservator fees, attorney fees, are all charged to your Estate (that's your money!). And these expenses go on year after year until you are restored to capacity or die (Probate 1860).

THE PROBLEMS

With all these perks, you may be ready to call your attorney to make an appointment to set up a Trust, but before doing so there are a few things you need to consider:

⊠   COMPLEXITY

A Trust is a fairly complex document, often 20 pages long. It needs to be that long because you are establishing a vehicle to take care of your property during your lifetime, as well as after your death. The Trust usually is written in "legalese," so it may take you considerable time and effort to understand it. It is important to have your Trust document prepared by an attorney who has the patience to work with you until you fully understand each paragraph of the document and are satisfied that what it says is what you really want.

⊠   COST

Because of the thoroughness of the document and the fact that it is custom designed for you, a Trust will cost much more to draft than a simple Will. In addition to the initial cost of the Trust, it can be expensive to maintain the Trust should you become disabled or die. Your Successor Trustee has the right to charge for his duties as Trustee, as well as to charge for any specialized services performed. A financial institution can charge to serve as Successor Trustee, and also charge to manage the Trust portfolio. If you decide to have a financial institution serve as Trustee, it is important that you compare fee schedules of different institutions.

You can choose an attorney to serve as Successor Trustee, but this may create a conflict of interest because the professional can use his position as Trustee to generate legal fees.

To prevent such abuse, the legislature passed a law stating that a Trustee who is an attorney may be paid only for his duties as Trustee. He may not be paid for legal services he provides on behalf of the Trust, nor can his law firm be paid for legal services — regardless of whether you made provision for legal fees in the Trust. If the Trustee has a parent, child, sibling or Spouse/RDP who is a lawyer, the prohibition extends to them as well (Probate 15687).

There are exceptions to the rule:
COURT PERMISSION
The attorney may give the beneficiaries of Trust written notice that he intends to pay himself for his duties as lawyer and as Trustee. Each beneficiary then has 30 days to give written notice of his objection to dual compensation. If an objection is raised, the Trustee/attorney can petition (ask) the Court to order that he be paid as attorney and also as Trustee (Probate 15687(d)).

ATTORNEY RELATIVE
The prohibition for dual compensation does not apply if your lawyer is your Spouse/RDP or is related to you through blood or marriage. Your relatives may be paid as attorney for your Trust and also as Trustee

You may decide to appoint your Spouse/RDP or a family member as Successor Trustee, who may want little, or no, compensation. Regardless of who you choose to be Successor Trustee, it is important that you include a provision for Trustee compensation. Your attorney can suggest different methods of compensation, such as a percentage of the principal value of the Trust and/or a percentage of income generated by the Trust property.

⊠ YOU MAY NEED YOUR SPOUSE/RDP'S PERMISSION TO TRANSFER PROPERTY INTO YOUR TRUST

Most couples prepare a Trust as part of their overall Estate Plan. Sometimes a married person or a Domestic Partner has a Trust that was prepared prior to the marriage, or he may decide to create a Trust to care for children from a previous marriage. The Grantor is free to place any of his Separate Property into the Trust, but he may not place Community Property into the Trust (or anywhere else not accessible to his Spouse/RDP) without the written consent of his Spouse/RDP (Family 1100).

If you are married and make a transfer of Community Property into your Trust without permission from your Spouse/RDP and that transfer results in your Spouse/RDP being deprived of a half interest in the Community Property, your Spouse/RDP has the right to ask the Court to undo the transfer and return his/her share of the Community Property. Your Spouse/RDP can petition the Probate Court at any time before or after your death. However, if your Spouse/RDP knows of the transfer and does nothing for three years, the Court could find that your Spouse/RDP failed to assert his/her rights in a timely manner and refuse to grant the petition (Family 1101).

⊠ PROBATE MIGHT STILL BE NECESSARY

The Trust only works for those items that you place in the Trust. Should you die owning property in your name only, Probate might be necessary in order to transfer the property to your beneficiary. For example, if you purchase a security in your name only, without a "Transfer On Death" designation to a named beneficiary or to your Trust, a Probate proceeding may be necessary to determine who should inherit the security.

The attorney who prepares the Trust creates a safety net for such situation. He prepares a Will for you to sign at the same time you sign the Trust. The Will makes your Trust the beneficiary of your Probate Estate. If you own anything in your name only and a Probate proceeding is necessary, the Will directs your Personal Representative to make that asset part of your Trust by transferring the asset to your Successor Trustee. Your Successor Trustee will add that asset to your Trust (Probate 6300).

The Will prepared by the attorney is called a *Pour Over Will* because it is designed to "pour" any asset titled in your name only, into the Trust. Having the Will ensures that all of your property will go to the beneficiaries named in your Trust. But the downside of holding property in your name only is that a full Probate administration may be necessary just to get that asset into your Trust. If avoiding Probate is your goal, holding property in your name only defeats that goal.

You can ensure that Probate will not be necessary by transferring your assets into your Trust during your lifetime, but if you neglect to put something into your Trust, the Pour Over Will stands by to transfer that asset into your Trust.

⊠ TAXES MAY STILL BE A PROBLEM

While you are operating the Trust as Trustee, all of the property held in your Revocable Living Trust is taxed as if you were holding that property in your own name. If the value of your Trust property exceeds the Estate Tax Exclusion value, taxes will be due once you die. If all you own is held in your Trust, your Successor Trustee will need to pay those taxes from the Trust property.

Those who have Estates large enough to incur Estate Taxes also need to think about how taxes will be paid on other taxable transfers. For example, suppose you and your brother bought a home as Joint Tenants With Right of Survivorship. If you each contributed equally to the purchase, and the property is now worth one million dollars, your brother will inherit your half million dollar share. If you also own two million dollars in other property all of which is in your Trust, your Taxable Estate is $2,500,000.

Unless your Trust directs otherwise, each beneficiary of your Estate is responsible to pay a proportionate share of the Estate Taxes. If federal Estate Taxes are reinstated so that anything over one million dollars is taxable at a rate of 40%, your Estate Tax will be $600,000. Your brother will need to contribute his prorated share of the Estate Taxes:

$$\$500,000 / \$2,500,000 = .2$$
$$20\% \text{ of } \$600,000 = \$120,000.$$

But suppose your brother doesn't have that kind of cash. Should he be forced to sell his home in order to pay the taxes? Should your Successor Trustee use your Trust property to pay your brother's taxes with a promise that he will reimburse the beneficiaries of your Trust at a later date? An experienced Estate Planning attorney can suggest any number of ways to head off such problems.

⊠ ☆ THE TRUST IS LEGALLY ENFORCEABLE

Your Successor Trustee will take over the administration of your Trust upon your incapacity or death. Should there be a dispute regarding the administration of the Trust, your beneficiary (or your Successor Trustee) can petition the Superior Court to settle the matter (Probate 17000). For example, your Successor Trustee is entitled to reasonable compensation. If you did not set the amount he is to be paid in the Trust Agreement and the beneficiaries object to the amount he is charging, they can ask the Court to determine his compensation.

We gave this section a cross and a star because the right to have a Trust enforced or administered by the Court is a double edged sword. It is great to have the Court protect the rights of your beneficiaries, but the cost of a court battle could be greater than if your Estate was Probated and the money simply distributed to your beneficiaries.

The beneficiaries of your Trust are at a financial disadvantage in a dispute with your Successor Trustee. The Court can require your Trustee to be personally liable for his legal costs, but that only happens if the Trustee acted illegally or unreasonably. In most cases, the Trustee will be able to charge the expense of defending his actions to your Trust and your beneficiaries will pay for their legal expenses out of their own pockets.

Win or lose, there will be just that much less for your beneficiaries to inherit.

Although all of the methods discussed in this Chapter can be used to transfer property without the need for Probate, each method may have a downside that is objectionable to you. Maybe you don't have enough money to warrant the cost of setting up the Trust at this time. Holding property jointly with another may raise issues of security and independence. Holding property so that it goes directly to a few beneficiaries in a Pay On Death account may not be as flexible as you wish. This may be the case if you wish to give gifts to several charities or to minor children instead of just one or two beneficiaries.

For example, if you hold all your property so that it goes to your son without the need for Probate, and you ask him to use some of the money for your grandchild's education, it may be that your grandchild gets none of the money because your son is sued or falls upon hard times. If you keep your property in your name only and leave a Will giving a certain amount of money for your grandchild, the child will know exactly how much money you left and the purpose of that gift.

After taking into account all the pros and cons of avoiding Probate, you may well opt for a Will and a Probate procedure. If you make such a decision, it is important to keep in mind that Estate Planning is not an "all or nothing" choice. You can arrange your Estate so that certain items pass automatically to your intended beneficiary, and other items can be left in your name only, to be distributed as part of a Probate procedure. By arranging your finances in this manner, you can reduce the value of your Probate Estate, and that in turn should reduce the cost of Probate.

Your California Will

Many people decide that the Will is the best route to go but do not act upon it, thinking it unnecessary to prepare a Will until they are very old and about to die. But according to reports published by the National Center for Health Statistics (a division of the U.S. Department of Health and Human Services) 2 of every 10 people who die in any given year are under the age of 60.

Twenty percent may seem like a small number until it hits close to home as it did with a young couple. They were having difficulty conceiving a child. They went from doctor to doctor until they met someone just beginning his practice. With his knowledge of the latest advances in medicine, he was able to help them.

The birth of their child was a moment of joy and gratitude. They asked a nurse to take a picture of them all together — the proud parents, the newborn child and the doctor who made it all possible. Happiness radiated from the picture, but within six months, one of them would be dead.

You might think it was the child. An infant's life is so fragile. SIDS and all manner of childhood diseases can threaten a little one. But no, he grew up a healthy young man.

If you looked at the picture, you might guess the husband. Overweight and stressed out; his ruddy complexion suggested high blood pressure. He looked like a typical heart-attack-prone Type A personality.

No, he was fine and went on to enjoy raising his son.

Probably it was the wife. She had such a difficult time with the pregnancy and the delivery was especially hard. Maybe it was all too much for her.

No, she recovered and later had two more children.

It was the doctor who was killed in a collision with a truck.

WHY A WILL IS NECESSARY

Though we all agree that one never knows, still people put off making a Will figuring that if they die before getting around to it, California law will take over and their property will be distributed in the manner that they would have wanted anyway. The problem with that logic is the complexity of California's Laws of Intestate Succession. If you are survived by a spouse, child, parent or sibling, it isn't too difficult to figure out who will inherit your property. But if none of these survive you, the ultimate beneficiary of your property may not be the person you would have chosen, had you taken the time to make a Will.

Others think that it is not necessary to have a Will because they arranged their finances so that all of their property will be inherited without the need for Probate. But money could come into your Estate after your death. This could happen in any number of ways. You might die in a house fire, or a flood. Your insurance company may need to pay for damages done to your home. You might be killed in a car accident caused by the wrongful act of someone. In such case, a Personal Representative may need to be appointed to sue on behalf of your Estate.

As explained in Chapter 6, without a Will, the Court will use the order of priority as set by California statute Probate 8461 to appoint a Personal Representative (see page 184). The person chosen by the Court may not be the person you would have chosen to settle your Estate. And as we will see in this Chapter, there are other important reasons to make a Will.

SET THE PERSONAL REPRESENTATIVE'S FEE

An important reason to make a Will is to choose your Personal Representative and to come to an understanding about how much compensation he/she is to receive. You can state that value in your Will.

 ### THE PERSONAL REPRESENTATIVE CAN SEEK MORE MONEY

Even though your Will states the amount of compensation to be given to your Personal Representative, if it is less than the statutory amount he may decide to ask the Probate Court to award a greater value (Probate 10802, 10831). If this is of concern to you, have your attorney draft an Agreement that you and your Personal Representative sign and incorporate into your Will. Having a separate fee Agreement will not stop your Personal Representative from asking for more money, but with such an Agreement, the Court will not agree to the increase unless something unusual occurs (such as a law suit) causing much more work than the ordinary Probate procedure.

You also need to keep in mind that the Personal Representative's fee is just to administer the Estate. It does not include payment for professional work he may do while settling the Estate. For example, if you appoint your attorney as Personal Representative, he can agree to the amount stated in the Will for his role as Personal Representative, and then ask the Court to award him attorney's fees as well. Under California law, he is entitled to receive compensation for both jobs, provided he asks the Court to be paid as a lawyer in advance, and the Court finds that the arrangement is to the advantage, benefit, and best interest of the Probate Estate (Probate 10804).

The same goes for any other professional. If you appoint your accountant to serve as Personal Representative, he is entitled to receive compensation for his work as Personal Representative. He will need to ask the Court to be paid for any accounting work he does such as preparing tax returns, preparing an inventory and doing an accounting for the beneficiaries. A financial planner who serves as Personal Representative may ask to be compensated for his management of the Estate property (buying and selling securities, taking care of rental property, etc.) in addition to his fee to administer the Estate.

But the main problem with appointing a professional as your Personal Representative is the same as appointing a professional to serve as the Successor Trustee of your Trust; namely, that it creates a potential conflict of interest. The professional can use his position as Personal Representative to generate fees that may not have been necessary if someone else settled the Estate.

When choosing a Personal Representative, consider the relationship of the Personal Representative to the beneficiaries and determine whether it would be better to appoint a non-professional for the job.

GIFT YOUR PERSONAL PROPERTY

Another benefit to making a Will is that you can make gifts of your personal property, including your car. If you make a gift of your car in your Will, it will be relatively simple for your car to be transferred to the beneficiary. If you do not make a *specific gift* of your car, it becomes part of your residuary Probate Estate. Your Personal Representative will decide what to do with the car. He can sell it and include the proceeds of the sale in the Estate funds to be distributed to your residuary beneficiaries; or he can give the car to a beneficiary of your Estate as part of that beneficiary's share of the Estate.

SMALL GIFTS MATTER

Many who have lost someone close to them report that the distribution of small personal items caused the greatest conflict. If you arrange your finances so that Probate is not necessary, your family will need to decide how to distribute your personal effects. Without guidance from you and no Personal Representative with authority to make decisions, there could be disagreement and hard feelings, over items of little monetary value. If you make a Will, you can include a list of gifts of personal effects in your Will and your Personal Representative will distribute the gifts according to your directions.

Of course, you cannot list each and every item you own, but you can instruct your Personal Representative to allow certain family members to take their choice of items not mentioned in your Will. If two or more family members want the same item, have your Personal Representative use an appropriate lottery system (coin toss, high card in a cut of a deck of cards, etc.) to decide who "wins."

GIFTS OF COMMUNITY PROPERTY

You can give only those items you own. If you are married or a Domestic Partner, unless you have an Agreement that states otherwise, personal property you acquire during your marriage is Community Property (Family 760). You can make a gift of Community Property, but only with the consent of your partner.

MAKE ADJUSTMENT FOR PRIOR GIFTS

You can use your Will to make adjustments for gifts or loans given during your lifetime. For example, if you loaned money to a family member and do not expect to be repaid, you can deduct the loan from that person's inheritance. There is no need to make the adjustment if the borrower gives you a promissory note because should you die, the money is owed to your Estate and the Personal Representative will deduct the balance owed from the borrower's inheritance. But if there is no evidence of the debt, and you neglect to make a Will, the borrower will receive whatever is allowed under the Laws of Intestate Succession (Probate 6409).

That was the case with Sally and her son. She and her husband Tom were firm believers in treating each of their four children equally. "Share and share alike" was their favorite saying. Once Tom died, Sally continued with the tradition, never giving to one child, without giving something of equal value, to each of the other three

Sally did not think of the loan she gave to her son as a gift. After all, he promised to pay it back — with interest! She did not ask her son to sign a promissory note. He was family. If you can't trust your son, who can you trust?

The son was prompt with his monthly payments. But only two payments had been made before his mother suddenly died from a heart attack. Sally never mentioned the loan to any of her other children. Neither did her son.

Each child received one quarter of their mother's Estate; and no one the wiser. Except whenever Sally's son dreams of his mother, she is not smiling.

⬚ MAKE PROVISION FOR BUSINESS INTERESTS

One of the most difficult Estates to settle is that of the decedent who owns and operates a small business. Does the Personal Representative transfer the business to a family member to continue in its operation? Should he try to sell the business, or maybe just liquidate its assets? Unless you make provision in your Will, those decisions will be made by your Personal Representative or the Probate Court. Under California law, the Personal Representative can continue the operation of the business for up to six months, without permission from the Court. After that he will need to get Court permission to continue to operate the business. Usually, the Court will set a hearing on the matter and have all interested parties express their opinion (Probate 9760).

All this legal hassle and expense can be avoided if you make specific provision in your Will for the operation and transfer of your business.

⬚ MAKE PROVISION FOR DEBTS AND TAXES

If money is owed on your car, home or other property, unless you make some other arrangement for the payment of the loan, the beneficiary of that item, will inherit the loan along with the gift (Probate 21131).

Taxes are another concern for those Estates large enough to be subject to Estate taxes. Federal and state law require that Estate Taxes be paid by the beneficiaries of the Estate in proportion to the value received, unless the decedent made some other arrangements to pay for the taxes (26 U.S.C. 6324 (a)(2), Probate 20110). If you make no provision for the payment of taxes, whoever inherits your property will pay a percentage of the Estate Taxes based on the amount they receive (Probate 20111).

If this is not as you wish, you can leave specific instructions setting aside funds to be used to pay debts and taxes. If you make arrangements to pay the debt from your Probate Estate, those who inherit property from a non-Probate transfer will not contribute to the payment of the debts and taxes. This means the amount inherited by the residuary beneficiaries of your Probate Estate will be reduced by the amount paid for your debts and taxes.

CHOOSE A GUARDIAN FOR YOUR CHILD
Each parent has the right to name someone in their Will to be Guardian of their child in the event that the parent dies before the child is grown, and the other parent is deceased (Probate 1500, 1502). Should the surviving parent die, whoever the parent named to serve as Guardian will have priority to be appointed as Guardian of the minor child. However, the judge will consider all of the factors before appointing a Guardian — including the child's choice of Guardian, provided the child is of sufficient age to form an intelligent preference His decision will be based on what he considers to be the best interest of the child (Probate 1513, 1514).

If you are leaving the child a significant amount of money, consider including a Trust as part of your Will. The person you appoint as Trustee will care for property left to the child until he is grown. Including a Trust in your Will, eliminates the need for the Court to appoint a Guardian of the child's property. You can choose the same person to serve as Trustee and as Guardian. If you name different people, the person you name as Guardian will care for the *person* of the child; i.e., he will make the child's medical, educational and religious training decisions. The person you name as Trustee will make financial decisions.

🗐 MAKE PROVISION FOR YOUR CHILD

You can "cut" your child (or anyone else for that matter) out of your Will by indicating that you intentionally make no provision for that child. If you wish to disinherit your child, simply omitting any reference to the child, may not be the best way to go. Your child may challenge the Will saying that you simply "forgot" to include the child as a beneficiary. It is best to discuss the problem with your attorney. He can suggest several provisions that can be included in your Will to avoid a challenge to your Will.

🗐 MAKE NO PROVISION FOR A NON-PROBATE ASSET

Property held in a Pay On Death Account, a Totten Trust Account, a car with a TOD designation, the proceeds of a life insurance policy, IRA accounts, etc. are all non-Probate assets because they are inherited by your named beneficiary without the need for Probate. You are free to change the beneficiary during your lifetime, but once you are deceased, the gift is made. You cannot change the beneficiary of such gift in your Will because you have, in effect, already made a gift of that asset (Probate 5304).

Unless you named your Estate as the beneficiary of a non-Probate asset, it should not even be mentioned in your Will. To do so might cause your Will to be challenged by whoever was named as the beneficiary of the non-Probate asset.

INCLUDE SAFEGUARDS FOR YOUR BENEFICIARIES

It is fairly common practice in California to include directions in a Will that the Personal Representative conduct the Probate procedure Independently. As explained in Chapter 6, even with an Independent Administration, he must still account to the Court for money spent. He must ask for Court permission to pay him or his attorney or to make distributions to the beneficiaries (Probate 10501).

Allowing the Personal Representative to act independently may save some time. It probably will not save any money because Personal Representative and attorney's fees are based on the value of your Estate. Still, you may want to allow an Independent Administration if you have only one or two beneficiaries, and they are on good terms with the Personal Representative. If you have significant real property, you may want him to have Limited Authority; i.e., he can act independently except for real estate transactions (Probate 10403).

You may be tempted to save money by asking that the Personal Representative serve without bond. However, a bond is protection for your beneficiaries. If the beneficiaries feel comfortable that their inheritance is safe, they are free to ask the Court to waive bond.

A Will may look like a simple document, but it takes a certain amount of legal expertise to write it in a manner that will be give effect to the wishes of the Will maker. A Will needs to be clearly worded. A sentence that can be read in two different ways can lead to a dispute over what you intended; and that could result in a long and expensive Court battle. Even though California Courts allow a Holographic (hand-scribed) Will to be admitted to Probate; it could be challenged in any number of ways, as explained in Chapter 5.

There is a statutory Will form included in Probate code 6240. If you want to prepare a Will without the assistance of an attorney, you can use that Will form. The statutory form is preceded by answers to frequently asked questions. The section is entitled: QUESTIONS AND ANSWERS ABOUT
THIS CALIFORNIA STATUTORY WILL

The section explains the meaning of legal terms used in the Will. If you wish to use the California statutory Will, it is best if you take the time to read sections 6200 through 6243 of the Probate Code. You can find these statutes at your local county law library or at the California statute Web site. http://www.leginfo.ca.gov/

Most importantly, it is important to have it signed and witnessed as described in the statute. If not, your Will may be challenged in any of the ways discussed in Chapter 5.

But if you are serious about having your property distributed exactly as you wish, it is best to have the document prepared by an attorney. He can explain California law to you so that your Will is less likely to be challenged.

Should someone say that you didn't know what you were doing when you made your Will, your attorney will be able to testify that the Will was prepared according to your specific instructions and that you were fully competent when you signed it.

STORING YOUR WILL

Once you sign your Will, you may wonder where to store it. Your attorney may suggest that he place it in his vault for safekeeping. By doing so, he ensures that your heirs will need to contact him as soon as you die. This does not mean that they are required to employ him should a Probate proceeding be necessary. It only means that he will have an opportunity for future employment.

But there are problems with such an arrangement. The Will could be lost or mistaken for another Will of a client who might happen to have the same name. That happened in at least one case. The attorney prepared Wills for two people with the same name and similar family circumstances. When one person died, the attorney submitted the wrong Will to Probate.

Luckily the error was quickly discovered. The decedent had a distinctive signature. The family challenged the validity of the Will based on the unfamiliar signature. They also challenged the way the property was to be distributed. They knew the decedent would never have made gifts in the manner stated in the Will.

If you decide to allow your attorney to store the Will, you need assurances that the attorney will be responsible for the document. You should get a receipt and something in writing that says:

⇨ The attorney accepts full responsibility for the storage of the Will. Should it be lost or damaged, he will redraft the document for you to sign, and at no cost to you. If you are deceased, he will, at no cost to your heirs, cooperate with the Court in an effort to have a valid copy of the lost or damaged Will accepted into Probate.

⇨ There will be no charge to you, or your heirs, for the storage and retrieval of the document.

⇨ Should he sell his practice, retire, or die, he or the successor to his practice, will notify you of the change and return the original document to you, at your request.

STORE IN SAFE DEPOSIT BOX

You might consider placing your Will in a safe deposit box that you lease at a bank. The only problem with the bank safe deposit box is convenient access. As we explained in Chapter 3, If you hold a safe deposit box in your name only, should you die, the bank will restrict access to the safe deposit box (Probate 331).

For those who are in a happy union, the solution to the problem of accessing the safe deposit box after death, may be to lease the box jointly with your Spouse/RDP such that each of you has free access to the box.

However, this may not be the best solution if you think your Spouse/RDP will be unhappy with certain provisions in your Will. Some Wills never see the light of day for this reason. In such case, it may be better to keep the safe deposit box in your name only. The bank may allow an inspection of your safe deposit box, under the supervision of an officer or employee of the company. The bank will allow your Will to be removed after making a copy of the document (Probate 331).

As explained in Chapter 7, those who have a Trust can solve the problem by giving their Successor Trustee joint access to the safe deposit box. If you are single and do not have a Trust, you can lease the box jointly with a trusted family member.

Of course, if privacy and security are important to you, this might offset any concern for the convenience of your beneficiaries. If so, consider keeping the document in a fireproof safe deposit box within your home. You can give a duplicate key to the person you chose to be your Personal Representative.

CHOOSING THE RIGHT ESTATE PLAN

Joint Ownership?
A Pay On Death bank account?
A Transfer On Death Security?
A Will?
A Trust?
A Life Insurance Policy???

Chapters 7 and 8 offer so many options that the reader may be more confused than when he was blissfully unenlightened.

As with most things in life, you may find there are no ultimate solutions, just alternatives. The right choice for you is the one that best accomplishes your goal. That means you first need to determine what you want to accomplish with the money you leave. Think about what will happen to your property if you were to die suddenly, without making any plan different from the one you now have.

Who will be responsible to pay your bills?
Who will inherit your property?
Will Probate be necessary?

If the answers to these questions are not as you wish, you need to spend time arranging your property to accomplish your goals.

For those with significant assets — especially those with Estates large enough to pay Estate Taxes, and for many others with special circumstances, e.g., blended families, or those with disabled family members, a trip to an experienced Estate Planning attorney may be well worth the consultation fee.

Your Estate Plan Record 9

Once you are satisfied with your Estate Plan, then the final thing to consider is whether your heirs will be able to locate your assets once you are gone.

Most people have their business records in one place, their Will in another place, car titles and deeds in still another place. When someone dies, their beneficiaries may feel as if they are playing a game of "hide and seek" with the decedent. The game might be fun were it not for the fact that an unlocated item may be forever lost. For example, suppose you die in an accident and no one knows you are insured by your credit card company for accidental death in the amount of $25,000. The only one to profit is the insurance company, which is just that much richer because no one told them that you died as a result of an accident.

And how about a key to a safe deposit box located in another state? Will anyone find it? Even if they find the key, how will they find the box?

It is not difficult to arrange things so that your affairs are always in order. It amounts to being aware of what you own (and owe) and keeping a record of your possessions. A side benefit is that by doing so, you will always know where all your business records are. If you ever spent time trying to collect information to file your taxes or trying to find a lost stock or bond certificate, you will appreciate the value of organizing your records.

ORGANIZING YOUR RECORDS

Heirs need all the help they can get. It's hard enough deal-ing with the loss, without the frustration of trying to locate important documents. Your heirs will have no problem locating your assets if you keep all of your records in a single place. It can be a file cabinet or a cardboard docu-ment box that you purchase from an office supply store. Organize your papers by placing them in separate folders such as:

📁 THE BANK & SECURITIES FOLDER

Store your original certificates for stocks, bonds, mutual funds, and certificates of deposit in a folder labeled **BANK & SECURITIES**. In addition to the origi-nal certificate, include a copy of the contract you signed with each financial institution. The contract will show where you have funds and who you named as beneficiary or joint owner of the account. If someone owes you money and signed a promis-sory note or mortgage identifying you as the lender, store these documents in this folder as well.

If you have a safe deposit box, keep a record of its location and the number of the box. Keep a copy of all of the items stored in the box in this folder. If you have an extra key to the box, put it here.

E-bank Accounts If you are doing your banking on-line, it is important to keep a record of your pass-words so that your family can access the account in the event of your incapacity or death. The same applies if you have on-line brokerage or installment loan accounts. Keep a paper record of these accounts in this folder.

📁 THE INSURANCE FOLDER

The **INSURANCE FOLDER** is for each insurance policy that you own, be it life insurance, homeowner's insurance, car insurance or a health care insurance policy. If you purchased real property, you probably received a title commitment at closing and an updated Abstract of Title or the title insurance policy some weeks later when you received your original deed from recording. If you cannot locate the title insurance policy, or Abstract contact the closing agent and have him send you a copy of your title policy.

📁 THE PENSION AND ANNUITY FOLDER

If you have a pension or annuity, put all of the documents relating to the pension in this folder. Include the telephone number and/or address of the person to contact in the event of your death.

FOR FEDERAL RETIREES If you are a federal retiree, you should have received your **PERSONAL IDENTIFICATION NUMBER (PIN)**. The person who will inherit your pension (your *survivor annuitant*) should have his own PIN as well. It is relatively simple to obtain your survivor's PIN during your lifetime, but it may be difficult and/or stressful for your survivor annuitant to work through the system once you are gone.

Survivor annuitant benefits are not automatic. Your survivor annuitant must apply for them by submitting a death claim to the Office of Personnel Management. Your survivor needs to know that it is necessary to apply and also how to apply. You can get printed information about how to apply for benefits from the Office Of Personnel Management (see page 38). Keep the printed information in this file.

📁 THE DEED FOLDER

Many people save every scrap of paper associated with the closing of real property. If you closed recently on real estate and there was a mortgage involved in the purchase, you probably walked away from closing with enough paper to wallpaper your kitchen. If you wish, you can keep all of those papers in a separate file that identifies the property, for example:

CLOSING PAPERS FOR THE SACRAMENTO PROPERTY

Place the original deed (or a copy, if the original is in a safe deposit box) in a separate **DEED FOLDER**. Include cemetery deeds, condominium deeds, cooperative shares to real property, timesharing certificates, deed to out of state property, etc. Also include a copy of related documents such as an Abstract of Title, or a recorded Condominium Approval. If you have a title insurance policy, put the original in the insurance folder, and a copy in this folder. If you have a mortgage on your property, put a copy of the recorded mortgage and promissory note in a separate **LIABILITY FOLDER**.

LOCATING REAL PROPERTY

If you own a vacant lot, your beneficiaries will find the deed (or a copy) in this folder but that deed will not contain the address of that property because it doesn't have one. The post office does not assign a street address until there is a building on the site. Your beneficiaries can get the location of the property from city or county records. But why make things hard for them? Include a handwritten note in this folder that tells them exactly how to locate the property.

📁 THE LIABILITY FOLDER

The LIABILITY FOLDER should contain all loan documents of money you owe. For example, if you purchased real property and have a mortgage on that property, put a copy of the mortgage and promissory note in this folder. If you owe money on a car, put the loan documents in this folder. If you have a credit card, put a copy of the contract you signed with the credit card company in this folder. A lease is a liability, because you contracted to pay a certain amount for the period of the lease, so include a copy of any lease agreement in this folder.

If you have a mortgage on your property, put a copy of the recorded mortgage and promissory note in this folder. Once the mortgage is paid off, within 30 days of the final payment, the lender needs to record a *Certificate of Discharge* in the county where the property is located and then instruct the Trustee of the Deed Trust to reconvey the property to you. Within 60 days, the Trustee should record a *Deed of Reconveyance* (Civil 2941).

You should receive your original promissory note, the recorded Certificate of Discharge and Deed of Reconveyance. Place those documents with the deed to the property. Remember to remove the paid mortgage from your Liability Folder.

Many people never take the time to calculate their net worth (what a person owns less what that person owes). By having a record of your assets and outstanding debts, you can calculate your net worth whenever you wish.

🗁 THE SEPARATE PROPERTY FOLDER

It is important for couples owning Community Property to keep a careful record of their ownership of Separate Property. If one partner is unable to pay his Separate Obligations, his creditors might suspect that property owned by the other partner is really Community Property and ask a Court to order an accounting. A careful record of the ownership of Separate Property may head off such investigation.

Married or single it is important to keep a record of your personal property in the event it is lost or stolen:

MOTOR VEHICLES Keep the title to all of your motor vehicle titles in this folder. This includes cars, mobile homes, boats, planes, etc. If you owe money on the vehicle, the lender may have possession of the title certificate. If such is the case, put a copy of the title certificate and registration in this folder and a copy of the loan documents in a separate liability folder. If you have a boat or plane, identify the location of the motor vehicle. For example, if you are leasing space in an airplane hangar or in a marina, keep a copy of the leasing agreement in this file.

JEWELRY If you own expensive jewelry, keep a picture of the item together with the sales receipt or written appraisal in this folder.

COLLECTOR'S ITEMS If you own a valuable art or coin collection, or any other item of significant value, include a picture of the item in this file. Also include evidence of ownership of the item, such as a sales receipt or a certificate of authenticity, or a written appraisal of the property.

📁 THE PERSONAL RECORDS FOLDER

The PERSONAL RECORDS FOLDER should include documents that relate to you personally, such as a birth certificate, naturalization papers, marriage certificate, Domestic Partnership registration, divorce papers, military records, Social Security card, etc. If you have a Power of Attorney or an Advance Health Care Directive, you can place the document in this folder, or in your Estate Planning folder. If you placed the original document in a safe deposit box, keep a copy in this folder together with the location of the original.

📁 THE ESTATE PLANNING DOCUMENT FOLDER

Place your Estate Planning documents (Will, Trust, Premarital or Pre-partnership Agreement, burial, funeral arrangements, etc.) in a separate folder. If your attorney has your original documents, or you placed the original in a safe deposit box, place a copy of the document in this folder together with instructions about how to find the original.

Regardless of where you store your Will or Trust, it is important to keep a copy of the document in your home. Over the years you may forget what provisions you made. Keeping a copy in your home may save you a trip to the safe deposit box to determine whether you need to update the document.

🗀 THE TAX RECORD FOLDER

Your Personal Representative (or next of kin) will need to file your final income tax returns. Keep a copy of your tax returns (both federal and state) for the past three years in your Tax Record Folder.

As explained in Chapter 2, beginning in 2010, there will be a cap on the step-up basis to 4.3 million dollars for property inherited by the spouse and 1.3 million dollars for property inherited by anyone else. It is important to keep a record of the basis of your property, not only for your heirs, but for yourself should you decide to sell the property during your lifetime. If you purchase real property, you need to keep a record of the purchase price as well as money you paid to improve the property. For condominium units, that will include special assessments for improvements to the condominium.

You will need these records to determine whether there will be a Capital Gains Tax on the transfer. Your accountant can help you set up a bookkeeping system to keep a running record of your basis in everything you own of value.

STORING YOUR FILES

The information stored in your files is important and may be difficult, if not impossible, to replace. Consider investing in a fire proof safe large enough to accommodate your files. Give a duplicate key to the safe to whomever you appointed as Personal Representative or Executor of your Estate.

THE *If I Die* FILE

Many do not have the time, nor inclination, to "play" with all these folders. They do not anticipate an immediate demise. Getting hit by a truck, or dying in a fiery plane crash is not something to think about, much less prepare for. But consider that death is not the only problem. You could take suddenly ill (say with a stroke) and become incapacitated. Even the most time-starved optimist should have a murmur of concern that his loved ones will be left with a mess should something unforeseen happen.

If you do not feel like doing a complete job of organizing your records at this time, consider an abridged version. You can set up a single file with a list of all you own and the location of each item. You need to make that file easily accessible to whomever you wish to manage your affairs in the event of your incapacity or death. You can do this by letting that person know of the existence of the file and how to get it in an emergency; or by keeping the file in an easily accessible place in your home with the succinct but attention-grabbing title of *"If I Die."*

We have included a form on the next page that you can use as a basis for information to be included in the file.

If I Die
the following information will help settle my Estate:

INFORMATION FOR DEATH CERTIFICATE
MY FULL LEGAL NAME _____

MY SOCIAL SECURITY NO. _____

BIRTH DATE AND BIRTH PLACE _____

If naturalized, date & place _____

MY FATHER'S NAME _____

MY MOTHER'S MAIDEN NAME _____

PEOPLE TO BE NOTIFIED
_____

_____

_____

FUNERAL AND BURIAL ARRANGEMENTS

LOCATION OF BURIAL SITE

_____

LOCATION OF PRENEED FUNERAL CONTRACT

_____

FOR VETERAN or SPOUSE BURIAL IN A NATIONAL CEMETERY

BRANCH_____SERIAL NO._____

VETERAN'S RANK _____

VETERAN'S VA CLAIM NUMBER _____

DATE AND PLACE OF ENTRY INTO SERVICE:
_____

DATE AND PLACE OF SEPARATION FROM SERVICE:
_____

LOCATION OF OFFICIAL MILITARY DISCHARGE
OR DD 214 FORM_____

LOCATION OF LEGAL DOCUMENTS

BIRTH CERTIFICATE _____

MARRIAGE CERTIFICATE_____

PREMARITAL AGREEMENT_____

DIVORCE DECREE _____

PASSPORT _____

WILL OR TRUST _____

DEEDS _____

MORTGAGES _____

TITLE TO MOTOR VEHICLES _____

POWER OF ATTORNEY _____

ADVANCE HEALTH CARE DIRECTIVE _____

Attorney name & telephone _____

LOCATION OF FINANCIAL RECORDS

INSURANCE POLICIES:

Name of Company, Location of Policy, Insurance Agent

_____

PENSIONS/ANNUITIES:

IF FEDERAL RETIREE: PIN NUMBER: _____

NAME OF SURVIVOR _____

SURVIVOR PIN NUMBER _____

BANK

Name and address of Bank, Account Number,
Location of Safe Deposit Box and Key

_____

_____

SECURITIES

Broker name and telephone number

_____

TAX RECORDS FOR PAST THREE YEARS

LOCATION _____

Accountant name and telephone number

_____

KEEPING UP TO DATE

We discussed people's natural disinclination to make an Estate Plan until they are faced with their own mortality. Many believe that they will make just one Will and then die (maybe that's why they put off making a Will). The reality is, most people who make a Will change it at least once before they die. If you have an Estate Plan, it is important to update it when any of the following events take place:

✍ **CHANGE IN MARITAL STATUS**
GETTING MARRIED
In the early 20th century, marriage was a simple thing. Two young people fell in love, and married. There was no need for a Premarital Agreement because they came to the marriage with little property and an intent to stay together "till death do us part." Today, young people postpone marriage until they have established careers, so they are coming into the marriage with property that they worked hard to acquire. The intent to remain married remains, but young people are realistic. They know the statistics. Half of the marriages don't work out. But, ever optimistic, the majority of those who divorce will marry at least once again, and in many cases, with children from a prior union.

It is a foolhardy couple who enter a relationship in today's society without an agreement that spells out the rights and responsibilities of the couple in the event that one of them dies, or they divorce. Courts in California will enforce the agreement, provided the document was prepared according to California law, i.e., the document was signed voluntarily after full disclosure of the finances of each party (Family 1615). A document that is too one-sided can be challenged in Court, so it is important that both parties be represented by their own attorney.

You should review your Premarital Agreement or Pre-partnership Agreement on a regular basis as your finances change or as you have children. With the consent of your spouse, you can amend your Agreement. If it needs a complete revision, you can revoke the agreement, and replace it with a Marital or Domestic Partnership Agreement (Family 1614). Changes to a Premarital or Pre-partnership Agreement should be prepared and signed in the same manner as with the original Agreement. There needs to be full disclosure by both parties as to the extent of their wealth. It is prudent that each party be represented by his own attorney.

If you do not have a Premarital or Pre-partnership Agreement, as explained at the end of Chapter 5, any Will you made before you married can be challenged by your surviving spouse. If successful, half of your Community Property and up to one-half of your Separate Property — depending on how much (s)he was entitled to inherit had you died without a Will (Probate 21610).

TERMINATING THE RELATIONSHIP
Under California law, should you divorce and then die before you get around to changing your Will, any gift that you made in your Will for your former spouse is revoked. Your Probate Estate will be distributed as if (s)he died before you (Probate 6122). A Registered Domestic Partner relationship is terminated by order of the Court or by filing a NOTICE OF TERMINATION OF DOMESTIC PARTNERSHIP with the California Secretary of State. As with a married couple any provision in the Will relating to the former Domestic Partner is revoked (Probate 6122.1).

SEPARATION HAS NO LEGAL EFFECT

You are free to live separately from your Spouse/RDP, but until and unless you make that separation permanent through divorce or termination, the law considers you to be married/Domestic Partners (Probate 6122). If you expect your separation will be permanent, you need to change your Will, Trust, insurance policies, etc. on your own. However, you will not be able to change title to real property that you own together with your Spouse/RDP, unless (s)he agrees to the change.

If you divorce or terminate a Domestic Partnership, you should change any Power of Attorney, or Health Care Directive appointing your spouse as your Agent. In addiion to changing the document, you need to let people know of the change. The law does not protect you if a transfer is made by someone who has not been so notified. If your former Spouse/RDP uses your Power of Attorney to sell your securities. You could sue your Spouse/RDP for doing so, but not your broker, unless you notified the broker that the Power of Attorney is revoked.

✍ A CHANGE IN RELATIONSHIP

If you marry, separate, divorce, have a child, or if a beneficiary of your Estate dies, you need to examine your Will to determine whether it needs to be revised. It is important to have changes made by a properly drafted and signed document. If you make changes by crossing things out or writing over your Will, the validity of the document can be challenged once you die. Simply ripping up the old Will effectively revokes the Will (Probate 6120). But it could happen that someone (perhaps your attorney) has a copy of the Will.

If no one knows that you revoked the Will, they may think the Will is lost and offer a copy of the Will for Probate (see page 92). Best to have a new Will prepared with the opening paragraph stating "I hereby revoke all prior Wills."

NOTIFY EMPLOYER OF CHANGE

If you change your marital status (either marry or divorce) you need to tell your employer of the change so that the employer can change your status for purposes of paycheck tax deductions. A health insurance or pension plan that provides benefits for a spouse, needs to be changed as well.

BENEFICIARY MOVES OR DIES

Most people remember to name an alternate beneficiary should one of their beneficiaries die. But how many of us remember to notify the pension plan or insurance company when a beneficiary moves? Many life insurance proceeds are never paid because the company cannot locate the beneficiary. The Actuarial Office of the Federal Employees' Group Life Insurance Program reported that as of September, 2003, they had over 55.8 million dollars in unpaid benefits, mostly because they could not locate the beneficiary at the last given address.

EXECUTOR/PERSONAL REPRESENTATIVE MOVES OR DIES

If your Executor dies before you do, and you have not named an alternate, you need to change your Will and do so. If your Executor moves out of state, consider appointing another who is a resident of California. It will be more convenient, and perhaps less expensive, to have someone who lives in California serve as your Personal Representative.

✍ RELOCATION TO A NEW STATE OR COUNTRY

There is no need to change your Estate Plan for a move within the state of California. If your attorney has your original Will, or any other of your original documents, then unless you intend to continue to employ him as your attorney, you need to retrieve your originals and take them with you.

There is much to check out if you move to another state or country. You need to determine whether your Will conforms to the laws of the state of your new residence. A Will that is signed and witnessed according the laws of the state, is generally accepted into Probate regardless of where it is drafted. However, many states will not accept an unwitnessed hand-written Will into Probate. If you have a Holographic Will, it is best to draft a new Will that conforms to the laws of the state of your new residence.

If you are married and have not provided the minimum amount as required by the laws of the new state, should you die before your spouse, your Will may be challenged on that basis. The same applies to a Trust. Most states allow a surviving spouse to demand funds from the Trust of the decedent spouse, if the deceased spouse did not provide the minimum amount to his spouse as required by the laws of that state.

MAKE PROVISION FOR SPOUSE/DP

You need to keep in mind that a California Domestic Partnership relationship is not recognized in most other states. Yet in all states, you can make provision for your Domestic Partner in a Will or Trust. You can also give your Domestic Partner authority to make your medical decisions and handle your finances in the event of your incapacity.

If you do not have a Will, it is important to check out the Laws of Intestate Succession for that state. In some states they are referred to as the *Laws of Descent and Distribution.* Each state has its own laws of inheritance and those laws vary state to state. Who has the right to inherit your property in the state of California may be different from who can inherit your property in another state. If you do not have a Will, this is the time to think about who will inherit your property should you die in the state of your new residence.

This is especially important for those who are married. There is a world of difference in the rights of a spouse in a Community Property state (Arizona, California, Idaho, Louisiana, Nevada, New Mexico, Texas, Washington and Wisconsin) and other states. There is even variation in the rights of a spouse from one Community Property state to another!

OTHER ESTATE PLANNING DOCUMENTS
A *Medical* or *Health Care Directive* is a document that gives instructions about the health care a person does (or does not) want to receive in the event that he is too ill to make his own health care decisions. In California, that document is called an *Advance Directive for Health Care.* The Directive can be used to appoint a *Health Care Agent* to carry out those directions (Probate 4701).

The form of a Health Care Directive varies significantly state to state. Other states may have laws that enable you to appoint someone with powers similar to a Health Care Agent, but the laws of the state may refer to such person as a *Patient Advocate* or a *Health Care Surrogate* or a *Health Care Representative*, with the right to make your health care decisions in the event that you are too ill to do so yourself.

It is best to have a Medical Directive using the forms and terms that are recognized in that state, rather than chance any confusion should you become ill and find yourself in an emergency situation.

Similarly, if you appointed someone to handle your finances under a Power of Attorney, you may want to have another prepared to conform to the laws of the new state, so there will be no question of the right of your Agent to conduct business on your behalf.

CREDITOR PROTECTION

Creditor protection is another item that is significantly different state to state. If you have much debt, determine what items can be inherited by your family free of your debts.

TAX CONCERNS

You also need to check out the taxes of the new state. Each state has its own tax structure. Some states have an inheritance tax, or a transfer tax on all inherited property. If state taxes are high, you may need an Estate Plan that will minimize the impact of those taxes.

When moving to another state you need to either educate yourself about the laws of the state, or consult with an attorney who can assist you in reviewing your Estate Plan to see if that plan will accomplish your goals in that state.

✍ CHANGE OF FORTUNE

Most of us do not have the good fortune of winning a lottery, nor the bad fortune of going bankrupt. However, we all have our ups and downs. It is important to review your finances every now and again to determine exactly what it is that you will be leaving to your beneficiaries. If you included a cash gift to a beneficiary, you need to be sure that your Probate Estate has enough money to make the gift. A Pay On Death account, or a Transfer On Death security will bypass Probate and be given directly to the beneficiary (Probate 5302, 5506). You may not include such accounts as part of your Will or Trust because you have already made a gift of those funds. If you wish to change the beneficiary of those accounts, you need to do so during your lifetime (Probate 5304).

✍ A SIGNIFICANT CHANGE IN THE LAW

A major problem associated with the legal system in the United States is its volatility. Changes might be easy to keep up with if we had only one set of laws. But we are ruled by federal statutes and regulations and state statutes and regulations. We pay state and federal legislators to make laws and change existing statutes and regulations. We pay judges to tell us the meaning of the law, but their interpretation of the law may change the way the law operates. The legislature and the judiciary do their job and so laws and regulations change frequently. Often without prior notice. We, the public, are charged with the duty of understanding the law. Many a citizen has been chided with "Ignorance of the law is no excuse."

Most of us have a general concept of what is, and what is not, allowed in our society. However, when presented with a particular problem, we may need to turn to a professional (lawyer, accountant, journalist, city official, etc.) for an explanation of the law.

Areas of the law that affect you and your family, personally, are discussed in this book, namely Probate Law, Tax Law, and Estate Planning (Wills and Trusts). It is important to keep up with news in these areas to learn about changes in the law that may affect your Estate Plan. It is a good idea to check with your attorney on a regular basis to determine whether you need to change your Will or Trust because of a change in state or federal law.

Also check out the Eagle Publishing Company Web site for update we will post to keep this book fresh.
http://www.eaglepublishing.com

GAMES DECEDENTS PLAY

We discussed the game of "hide and seek" some decedents play with their heirs. A variation of that game is the "wild goose chase." The person who plays this game is one who never updates his files. His records are filled with all sorts of lapsed insurance policies, promissory notes of debts long since paid, brokerage statements of securities that have been sold, and so on.

When he is gone, his family will become frustrated as they try to hunt down the "missing" asset. If you wish to play this game, then the best joke is to keep the key to a safe deposit box that you are no longer leasing. That will keep folks hunting for a long time!

If you do not have a wicked sense of humor, do your family a favor and update your records on a regular basis.

Glossary

ABSTRACT OF TITLE An *Abstract of Title* is a condensed history of the title to real property. It consists of a summary of all the recorded documents, including mortgages, that affect title to a given parcel of land.

ADMINISTRATION The *Administration* of a Probate Estate is the management and settlement of the decedent's affairs. There are different types of administration. See *Ancillary Administration.*

ADMINISTRATIVE LAW JUDGE An *Administrative Law Judge* is someone who is appointed to conduct an administrative hearing. He has the power to administer oaths, take testimony, and then decide the facts of the case. Although he can decide the facts of the case, the final outcome of the hearing is decided by the government agency that appointed the Administrative Law Judge.

ADVANCE HEALTH CARE DIRECTIVE An *Advance Health Care Directive* is a document that gives directions about the type of health care the person signing the document (the Principal) wants in the event he is too ill to speak for himself.

AFFIANT An *Affiant* is someone who signs an affidavit and swears or acknowledges that it is true in the presence of a notary public or other person with authority to administer an oath or take acknowledgments.

AFFIDAVIT An *Affidavit* is a written statement of fact made by someone voluntarily, under oath, or acknowledged as being true, in the presence of a notary public or someone else who has authority to administer an oath or take acknowledgments.

AGENT   An *Agent* is someone who is authorized by another (the *principal*) to act for, or in place of, the principal.

ANATOMICAL GIFT An *Anatomical Gift* is the donation of all or part of the body of the decedent for the purpose of transplantation or research.

ANCILLARY ADMINISTRATION An *Ancillary Administration* is a Probate proceeding that aids or assists the original (primary) Probate proceeding. Ancillary administration is conducted to determine the beneficiary of the decedent's property located within that state, and to determine whether the property is taxable in that state.

ANNUAL GIFT TAX EXCLUSION The *Annual Gift Tax Exclusion* is the amount a person can gift to another each year without being required to file a federal Gift Tax Return. The Gift Tax Exclusion for the year 2007 is $12,000.

ANNUITANT   An *annuitant* is someone who is entitled to receive payments under an annuity contract.

ANNUITY An *annuity* is a contract that gives someone (the annuitant) the right to receive periodic payments (monthly, quarterly) for the life of the annuitant or for a given number of years.

ASSET An *asset* is anything owned by someone that has a value, including personal property (jewelry, paintings, securities, cash, motor vehicles, etc.) and real property (condominiums, vacant lots, acreage, residences, etc.).

ASSIGN To *assign* is to transfer one's rights in or to something to another. For example, a contract may allow a party to assign his rights in the contract to another person.

ATTORNEY or ATTORNEY AT LAW An *attorney*, also known as an *Attorney at law*, or a *lawyer*, is someone who is licensed by the state to practice law in that state.

ATTORNEY-IN-FACT An *Attorney-In-Fact* is someone appointed to act as an Agent for another (the *Principal*) under a Power of Attorney.

BASIS The *basis* is a value that is assigned to an asset for the purpose of determining the gain (or loss) on the sale of the item or in determining the value of the item in the hands of someone who has received it as a gift.

BENEFICIARY A *beneficiary* is one who benefits from the act of another or from the transfer of property. In this book we refer to a beneficiary as someone named in a Will, Trust, or deed to receive property, or someone who inherits property under the Laws of Intestate Succession.

BOND A *bond* required by the Probate Court is a written document that guarantees the Personal Representative will perform his duties as required by law. The person or company that insures the performance of the Personal Representative is called a *surety.* The value of the bond is set by the Court. The cost of purchasing the bond is charged to the decedent's Estate.

CAPITAL GAINS TAX A *Capital Gains Tax* is a tax on the amount the net sales proceeds exceeds the basis of a capital asset sold by a taxpayer.

CAVEAT *Caveat* is Latin for "Let him beware." It is a warning for the reader to be careful.

CFR   *CFR* is the abbreviation for the *United States Code of Federal Regulations.*

CLAIM A *claim* against the decedent's Estate is a demand for payment of a debt of the decedent. To be effective, the claim must be filed with the Probate Court within the time limits set by law.

CODE A *Code* is a body of laws arranged systematically for easy reference e.g. the Internal Revenue Code.

CODICIL A *Codicil* to a Will is a supplement or an addition to a Will that changes certain parts of the Will.

COLUMBARIUM A *Columbarium* is a separate room or building with niches (spaces) designed to store urns containing the ashes of cremated bodies.

COMMISSION A *commission* is compensation paid to someone for performing a service.

COMMISSIONER A *Commissioner* is someone appointed by the Court or by the government to do a job.

COMMON LAW MARRIAGE A *Common Law marriage* is one that is entered into without a state marriage license or any kind of official marriage ceremony. A Common Law marriage is created by an agreement to marry, followed by the two living together, and telling everyone they know that they are husband and wife. California does not recognize such a marriage as being valid when entered into within the state of California.

COMMUNITY PROPERTY STATE Certain states (Arizona, California, Idaho, Louisiana, Nevada, New Mexico, Texas, Washington, and Wisconsin) have laws stating that property acquired by husband or wife, or both, during their marriage is *Community Property* and is owned equally by both of them.

COMMUNITY PROPERTY ACCOUNT A *Community Property Account* is an account owned by a married couple. Should one of them die, half of the account becomes the property of the surviving spouse. The other half is distributed according the decedent's Will or Trust; or if neither of these, then according to the Laws of Intestate Succession.

COMMUNITY PROPERTY WITH RIGHT OF SURVIVORSHIP *Community Property With Right of Survivorship* is a method of ownership created by the California legislature that enables a married couple to own property with the right of the spouse to inherit the property without going through a Probate procedure, while preserving the Community status of the property, i.e., enabling the surviving spouse to take a step-up in basis of the entire value of the property.

CONSERVATOR A *Conservator* is someone appointed by the Superior Court to manage, protect and preserve the property of someone who is missing, or an adult who the Court finds is unable to care for his property because of his incapacity.

CONTINGENT BENEFICIARY A *Contingent Beneficiary* is someone (an *Alternate Beneficiary*) who may, or will, benefit if the primary beneficiary dies or otherwise loses rights as a beneficiary.

CONFLICT OF INTEREST A *conflict of interest* is a conflict between the official duties of a fiduciary (Guardian, Trustee, attorney, etc.) and his own private interest. For example, it is a conflict of interest for a Successor Trustee to use Trust property for his own personal profit.

CORONER A **Coroner** is a public official who makes inquiry into the cause of a death that occurs under unnatural or suspicious circumstances. In many counties, the Coroner's duties are performed by a public official with the title of *Medical Examiner*.

COURT The **Court** as used in this book is the Probate Court. When referring to an order made by the court, the term is synonymous with "judge," i.e., an "order of the court" is an order made by the judge of the court.

CREDITOR A **creditor** is someone to whom a debt is owed by another person (the *debtor*).

CREMAINS **Cremains** is shorthand for **cremated remains**. It refers to the ashes of a person who was cremated.

CURTESY **Curtesy** is the right of a husband, upon the death of his wife, to a life estate in real property she owned during their marriage, provided they had a surviving child who could inherit the property. This English Common Law has been abolished in most states, including California.

CUSTODIAN A **Custodian** under California's **Uniform Transfers to Minors Act** is a person or a financial institution that accepts responsibility for the care and management of property given to a minor child.

DAMAGES **Damages** is money that is awarded by a Court as compensation to someone who has been injured by the action of another.

DEBTOR A **debtor** is someone who owes payment of money or services to another person (the *creditor*).

DECEDENT The *Decedent* is the person who died.

DEED OF TRUST A *Deed of Trust* is a deed that places title to real property in Trust to secure payment of monies owed on the property. It serves the same function as a mortgage. Once the debt is paid the Trustee will execute a *Deed of Reconveyance* returning title to the property back to the borrower.

DESCENDANT A *descendant* is someone who descends from a common ancestor. There are two kinds of descendants: a *lineal descendant* and a *collateral descendant*. The lineal descendant is one who descends in a straight line such as father to son to grandson. The collateral descendant is one who descends in a parallel line, such as a cousin. In this book, unless otherwise stated, the term *descendant* refers to a *lineal descendant*.

DESIGNATED AGENT A *Designated Agent* of a corporation is someone who is authorized to act on behalf of the company and accept service of process in the event the company is sued.

DISTRIBUTION The *distribution* of a Trust or Probate Estate is the giving to the beneficiary that part of the Estate to which the beneficiary is entitled.

DMV *DMV* is the abbreviation for the California Department of Motor Vehicles.

DOMESTIC PARTNERS California statute defines *Domestic Partners* as two adults who have chosen to share one another's lives in an intimate and committed relationship of mutual caring (Family 297)

DOWER *Dower* is the right of a wife, upon the death of her husband, to a Life Estate in one-third of all real property that he owned during their marriage. This English Common Law has been abolished in most states, including California.

DURABLE POWER OF ATTORNEY A *Durable Power of Attorney* is a document in which the person who signs the document (the *Principal*) gives another person (his *Attorney in Fact*) authority to do certain things on behalf of the Principal. The Attorney in Fact is also referred to as the Principal's *Agent*. The word *"durable"* means that the authority of the Agent continues even if the Principal is incapacitated at the time that the Agent is acting on behalf of the Principal.

DURABLE POWER OF ATTORNEY FOR HEALTH CARE A *Durable Power of Attorney for Health Care* is a Durable Power of Attorney that gives the Attorney In Fact authority to make medical decisions for the Principal.

ENCUMBRANCE An *encumbrance* is a claim or a lien or a liability that is attached to real property, such as a mortgage, or lease or a mechanic's lien.

EQUITABLE *Equitable* is whatever is right or just. If property is distributed to two or more people equitably, then the division is not necessarily equal, but according to the principles of justice or fairness.

EQUITY The *equity* in a home is the market value of the home less monies owed on the property (mortgages, tax liens, etc.).

ERISA **ERISA** is the abbreviation for the Employee Retirement Income Security Act. This federal law governs the funding, investment, administration and termination of private pension plans.

ESTATE A person's *Estate* is all of the property (both real and personal property) owned by that person. The decedent's Estate may also be referred to as his *Taxable Estate* because all of the decedent's assets must be included when determining whether Estate Taxes are due. Compare to PROBATE ESTATE.

EXECUTOR An *Executor* (feminine *Executrix*) is a legal term found in many Wills. The terms refer to the person appointed by the Will maker to carry out directions given in the Will. In modern Wills, this term has been replaced by *Personal Representative.*

FAIR MARKET VALUE The *Fair Market Value* of a home is the amount at which the property would change hands between a willing buyer and seller, both having reasonable knowledge of the facts.

FAMILY ALLOWANCE The *Family Allowance* is the amount set aside by the Probate Court to pay for the support and maintenance of the decedent's surviving Spouse/RDP and dependents during the year following his death.

FIDUCIARY A *Fiduciary* is one who takes on the duty of holding property in Trust for another or acting for the benefit of another, such as a Personal Representative, Trustee, Guardian etc.. A fiduciary relationship is also one that is developed out of trust and confidence. For example, an attorney has a fiduciary relationship with his client.

FRATERNAL BENEFIT SOCIETY A *Fraternal Benefit Society* is a not-for-profit society or voluntary association that is organized to accomplish some worthy civic goal, and for the mutual benefit of its members.

GRANTEE   The *Grantee* of a deed is the person who receives title to real property from the *Grantor*.

GRANTOR The *Grantor* is someone who transfers property. The Grantor of a deed is the person who transfers real property to a new owner (the Grantee). The Grantor of a Trust is someone who creates the Trust and then transfers property into the Trust. Also see SETTLOR.

GUARANTOR A *Guarantor* is someone who promises to pay a debt or perform a contract for another person in the event that person does not fulfill his obligation.

GUARDIAN in California, a *Guardian* is someone who has legal authority to care for the person and/or property of a minor.

HEALTH CARE AGENT   A *Health Care Agent* is someone who is appointed by another (the *Principal*) to make medical decisions on behalf of the Principal, in the event the Principal is unable speak for himself.

HEALTH CARE DIRECTIVE A *Health Care Directive* is a statement made by someone (the principal) in the presence of witnesses or a written, notarized statement in which the principal gives directions about the care he/she wishes to receive. See *Living Will*.

HOLOGRAPHIC WILL A *Holographic Will* is a Will written, dated and signed by the hand of the Will maker himself. A Holographic Will may be admitted into Probate in California, however many states refuse to accept a Holographic Will unless it is witnessed according to the laws of the state.

HOMESTEAD The *homestead* is the dwelling and land owned and occupied as the owner's principal residence.

HEIR   An *heir* is anyone entitled to inherit the decedent's property under the Laws of Intestate Succession OR LAWS OF DESCENT in the event that the decedent dies without a Will.

INCAPACITATED   The term *incapacitated* is used in two ways: a person is *physically incapacitated* if he has a physical disability. A person is *legally incapacitated* if a Court finds that a person is unable to care for his person or property. Once a judge determines that a person is legally incapacitated, he will appoint someone to care for the person and/or property of the incapacitated person.

INDIGENT A person who is *indigent* is one who is poor and without funds.

INSOLVENT A person or business is *insolvent* if more money is owed than owned, or if the person or business is unable to pay debts as they come due.

INTER VIVOS TRUST An *Inter Vivos Trust* (also known as a *Living Trust*) is a Trust that is created and becomes effective during the lifetime of the Grantor (or Settlor) as opposed to a Trust that he includes as part of his Will to take effect upon his death.

INTESTATE *Intestate* means not having a Will or dying without a valid Will. *Testate* is dying with a valid Will.

IRA ACCOUNT An *Individual Retirement Account ("IRA")* is a retirement savings account in which income taxes on certain deposits and interest to the account are deferred until the monies are withdrawn.

IRREVOCABLE TRUST An *Irrevocable Trust* is a Trust that cannot be changed, cancelled or terminated until its purpose is accomplished.

ISSUE The decedent's *issue* are his descendants, children, grandchildren, great-grandchildren, etc. See DESCENDANT.

JOINT AND SEVERAL LIABILITY If two or more people agree to be *jointly and severally liable* to pay a debt, then each individually agrees to be responsible to pay the debt, and together they all agree to pay for the debt.

JOINT TENANCY In California, a *Joint Tenancy* means that each tenant owns an equal share of the property with right of survivorship; i.e., should one Joint Tenant die the remaining tenants own the property.

KEY MAN INSURANCE *Key man insurance* is an insurance policy designed to protect a company from economic loss in the event that an important employee of the company becomes disabled or dies.

KEOGH PLAN A *Keogh Plan* is a retirement plan available to self-employed taxpayers. Certain tax benefits are available such as tax deductions for annual contributions to the plan. The plan is named for its author, Eugene James Keogh.

LAWS OF INTESTATE SUCCESSION *The Laws of Intestate Succession* are the laws of the state that determine who is entitled to inherit the decedent's Probate Estate when he dies without a valid Will.

LEGALESE *Legalese* refers to the use of legal terms and confusing text that is used by some attorneys to draft legal documents.

LESSOR A *Lessor* is a person or company who leases property to another (the *Lessee*). In the case of real property, the Lessor is known as the Landlord and the Lessee as the Tenant.

LETTERS *Letters* is a document, issued by the Probate court, giving the Personal Representative authority to take possession of and to administer the Estate of the decedent.

LIEN A *lien* is a charge against a person's property as security for a debt. The lien is evidence of the creditor's right to take the property as full or partial payment, in the event that the debtor defaults in paying the monies owed.

LIFE ESTATE A *Life Estate* interest in real property is the right to possess and occupy the property for so long as the owner of the Life Estate lives. When the owner of the Life Estate dies, the property will belong to the owner of the *Remainder Interest*.

LITIGATION *Litigation* is the process of carrying on a lawsuit, i.e., to sue for some right or remedy in a court of law. A Litigation Attorney is one who is experienced in conducting the law suit and in particular, going to trial.

LIVING WILL A *Living Will* is a Health Care Directive that gives instructions about whether life support systems should be withheld or withdrawn in the event that the person who signs the Living Will is terminally ill or in a persistent vegetative state and unable to speak for himself.

MARITAL AGREEMENT A *Marital Agreement* is an agreement made by a couple after marriage to decide their respective rights in case of a dissolution or the death of a spouse.

MEDICAID *Medicaid* is a public assistance program sponsored jointly by the federal and state government to provide Medical Assistance for people with low income and limited assets. In California, it is called *Medi-Cal*.

MEDI-CAL See MEDICAID.

MOBILE OR MANUFACTURED HOME A *mobile* or *manufactured home* is a structure that is built on a permanent chassis (i.e. supporting frame). It is transportable in one or more sections. It is designed for use as a dwelling with provision made for connection to utilities.

NET CONTRIBUTION The decedent's *net contribution* to a bank account is the amount he deposited, less the amount he withdrew, plus a pro rata share of interest deposited to the account as of the decedent's date of death.

NET PROBATE ESTATE The *Net Probate Estate* is the value of the decedent's Probate Estate, less all the monies paid to settle the Estate, i.e. what is left once all valid claims and the costs and expenses of the Probate procedure are paid.

NET PROCEEDS The *net proceeds* of a sale is the sale price less costs and expenses paid to make the sale.

NET WORTH A person's *net worth* is the value of all of the property that he owns less the monies he owes.

NEXT OF KIN *Next of kin* has two meanings in law: *next of kin* refers to a person's nearest blood relation or it can refer to those people (not necessarily blood relations) who are entitled to inherit the property of a person under the Laws of Intestate Succession.

NON-PROBATE TRANSFER A *Non-probate Transfer* is the transfer of property to the decedent's beneficiary without the necessity of a Probate Procedure. This includes property that is transferred to the surviving joint owner, or property transferred to the beneficiary of a Pay On Death account.

PERJURY *Perjury* is lying under oath. The false statement can be made as a witness in court or by signing an Affidavit. Perjury is a criminal offense.

PERSONAL EFFECTS *Personal effects* is personal property that is kept for one's personal use such as clothing, jewelry, books, and other items generally found in the home.

PERSONAL PROPERTY *Personal property* is all property owned by a person that is not real property (real estate). It includes personal effects, cars, securities, bank accounts, insurance policies, etc.

PERSONAL REPRESENTATIVE A *Personal Representative* is someone appointed by the Probate Court to settle the decedent's Estate and to distribute whatever is left to the proper beneficiary.

PER CAPITA *Per Capita* is a method of distributing property to a group of beneficiaries such that the share intended for a beneficiary who dies before the gift is distributed goes to the remaining beneficiaries.

PER STIRPES *Per Stirpes* is a method of distributing property to a group of beneficiaries. In the event a beneficiary dies before the gift is distributed, the deceased person's share goes to his descendants. If he has no descendants, the surviving beneficiaries share equally in the gift.

PETITION A *Petition* is a formal written request to a Court asking the Court to take action or issue an order on a given matter; e.g. a request to appoint a Guardian.

POWER OF ATTORNEY A *Power of Attorney* is a document in which someone (the *Principal*) gives another person (his *Agent* or *Attorney In Fact*) authority to do certain things on behalf of the Principal.

PREMARITAL AGREEMENT A *Premarital Agreement* (also known as an *Antenuptial* or *Prenuptial Agreement*) is an agreement made prior to marriage whereby a couple provides for the management of the property during marriage and how their property is to be divided should one die, or they later divorce.

PRINCIPAL The *Principal* of a Power of Attorney is the person who permits or directs another (his *Attorney-In-Fact* or *Agent*) to act for him.

PROBATE *Probate* is a Court procedure in which a Court determines the existence of a valid Will. The decedent's Estate is then settled by the Personal Representative who pays all valid claims and then distributes whatever remains to the proper beneficiary.

PROBATE ESTATE The *Probate Estate* is that part of the decedent's Estate that is subject to Probate. It includes property that the decedent owned in his name only or as a Tenant In Common. It does not include property that was owned jointly with right of survivorship, or in trust for another.

PRO BONO The term *Pro Bono* means "for the public good." When an attorney works Pro Bono, he does so voluntarily and without pay.

PROPRIETARY LEASE A *Proprietary Lease* is a lease giving the tenant the exclusive, legal, right to occupy the apartment. See CO-OP.

PUNITIVE DAMAGES *Punitive damages* are awarded by a Court to punish someone who deliberately disregarded the rights or safety of another. It is money awarded in addition to *compensatory damages* which are monies awarded to reimburse the wronged person for actual losses.

QRP *QRP* is the abbreviation for a *Qualified Retirement Plan.* It is a retirement plan that qualifies for certain federal income tax deferrals or credits.

REAL PROPERTY *Real property,* also known as *real estate,* is land and anything permanently attached to the land such as buildings and fences.

REGISTERED DOMESTIC PARTNERSHIP A *Registered Domestic Partnership* is a relationship established by the California legislature. The Partnership is established when a couple, who meet the criteria established by statute (i.e., a common residence, at least 18, not related by blood or marriage, etc.) .file a *Declaration of Domestic Partnership* with the California Secretary of State (Family 297).

REMAINDER INTEREST The *Remainder Interest* in real property is the property that passes to the owner of that Interest, once the owner of the Life Estate dies. See LIFE ESTATE

RESIDUARY BENEFICIARY A *Residuary Beneficiary* of a Will is a beneficiary who is entitled to whatever is left of the Probate Estate once specific gifts made in the Will have been distributed and the decedent's bills, taxes and costs of Probate have been paid.

RESIDUARY ESTATE The *Residuary Estate* is that part of the Probate Estate that is left after all the debts, taxes, and costs of administration are paid and specific gifts distributed.

REVOCABLE TRUST   A *Revocable Trust* is a Trust which can be amended or revoked by the Settlor during his lifetime.

REVOCABLE LIVING TRUST A *Revocable Living Trust* (also known as an *Inter Vivos Trust*) is a Revocable Trust that is created and becomes effective during the lifetime of the Settlor.

RIGHT OF SURVIVORSHIP A *Right of Survivorship* is the right of the survivor of a deceased person to property owned by the decedent.

SECURED LOAN A *secured loan* is a loan backed by property. If the borrower does not pay the loan, the lender can take the property. Car loans and mortgages are secured debts.

SELF PROVED WILL A *Self Proved Will* is a Will that eliminates some of the formalities of proof in a Probate procedure. The Will is Self Proved if signed by the witnesses in the form as required by the statute.

SEPARATE PROPERTY In California, the term *Separate Property* refers to property that is owned by a married person in his/her own right. It includes property owned by the person prior to marriage, as well as inheritances and gifts received by the person during the marriage.

SETTLOR   A *Settlor* Is someone who creates and then funds a Trust.

SIBLING   A *sibling* is one of two or more people born of the same parents; i.e., a brother or a sister. Unless, otherwise noted, we used the term to include those who have only one parent in common; i.e. a half brother or a half sister.

SOLEMNIZE   To *solemnize* a marriage is to enter a marriage publicly, before witnesses, rather than privately as in a common law marriage.

SPECIFIC GIFT A *Specific Gift* is a gift of a specific item, or part of the Will maker's Estate, that is made to a named beneficiary of the Will.

SPENDTHRIFT   A *spendthrift* is someone who spends money carelessly or wastefully or extravagantly.

SPENDTHRIFT TRUST   A *Spendthrift Trust* is a Trust created to provide monies to a beneficiary, and at the same time protect the Trust property from being taken by the creditors of the beneficiary.

SPOUSE/RDP *Spouse/RDP* is the abbreviation for "Spouse or Registered Domestic Partner."

SSI *SSI* Is the abbreviation for *Supplemental Security Income*, a federal benefit given to qualified disabled persons

STATUTE OF LIMITATION A *Statute of Limitation* is a federal or state law that sets maximum time periods for taking legal action. In general, no legal action can be taken once the time set out in the statute passes.

STEPPED-UP BASIS A *stepped-up basis* is the fair market value placed on property that is purchased or inherited from another. The "step-up" refers to the increase in value from the basis of the former owner (usually what he paid for it), to the basis of the new owner (usually the market value when the transfer is made).

STOCK COOPERATIVE A *Stock Cooperative* is an apartment in a multi-dwelling complex. The complex is usually organized as a corporation. Each owner has an interest in the entire complex, usually in the form of a share of stock in the corporation. Unlike a condominium, he does not own his own apartment, but rather he has as *Proprietary Lease* to his apartment. See PROPRIETARY LEASE.

SUPERIOR COURT Each county in California has a *Superior Court*. Probate is conducted in the Probate division of the Superior Court.

SUCCESSOR TRUSTEE A *Successor Trustee* is someone who takes the place of the Trustee.

SURROGATE A *Surrogate* is a substitute; someone who acts in place of another.

TENANCY IN COMMON *Tenancy In Common* is a form of ownership such that each Tenant owns his share without any claim to that share by the other owners. There is no right of survivorship. Should a Tenant In Common die, his share belongs to his Estate and not to the surviving owners.

TESTATE *Testate* means to die with a valid Will.

TESTATOR A *Testator* (feminine *Testatrix*) is someone who makes and signs a Will; or someone who dies leaving a Will.

TITLE INSURANCE *Title Insurance* is a policy issued by a title insurance company after searching title to the property. The insurance covers losses that result from a defect of title, such as unpaid taxes, or a claim of ownership of the property.

TOTTEN TRUST ACCOUNT A *Totten Trust Account* is a bank account that is held in trust for a beneficiary. The terms of the Trust are established through agreement with the bank, and not through a separate Trust Agreement.

TRUST AGREEMENT A *Trust Agreement* is a document in which someone (the Settlor or Trustor) creates a Trust and appoints a Trustee to manage property placed into the Trust. The usual purpose of the Trust is to benefit persons or organizations named by the Settlor as beneficiaries of the Trust.

TRUSTEE A *Trustee* is a person, or institution, who accepts the duty of managing Trust property for the benefit of another.

TENANCY BY THE ENTIRETY A *Tenancy by the Entirety* is a form of ownership of real property held by a husband and wife. It is a joint tenancy with right of survivorship, modified by the Common Law concept that the husband and wife are one. With a Tenancy by the Entirety, each owns 100% of the property both before and after death. California, being a Community Property state does not recognize this form of ownership.

UNDUE INFLUENCE   *Undue influence* is pressure, influence or persuasion that overpowers a person's free will or judgment, so that a person acts according to the will or purpose of the dominating party.

UNSECURED CREDITOR An *unsecured creditor* is someone who is owed money on a promissory note with nothing to back it up if payment is not made. A *secured creditor* holds some special assurance of payment, such as a mortgage on real property or a lien on a car.

VOID GIFT A *void gift* is one that is not legally enforceable. For example, if a Will makes a gift and the Court finds that provision to be void, the beneficiary has no legal right to receive that gift.

WAIVER   A *waiver* is the intentional and voluntary giving up of a known right.

WRONGFUL DEATH   A *wrongful death* is a death that was caused by the willful or negligent act of a person or company.

INDEX

STATUTES, FEDERAL
CODE OF FEDERAL
  REGULATIONS ("CFR")
  40 CFR 229.1   20

FEDERAL TRADE COMMISSION
  RULES ("FTC")
  453.2   15, 16
  453.3   18
  453.4   16
  453.5   16

UNITED STATES CODE ("U.S.C.")
  26 U.S.C. 121   45
  26 U.S.C. 1022   44
  26 U.S.C. 2503   41

STATUTES, FEDERAL
UNITED STATES CODE ("U.S.C.")
  26 U.S.C. 6075   41
  26 U.S.C. 6324   234
  28 U.S.C. 1738   138
  29 U.S.C. 1162   56
  29 U.S.C. 1163   56
  29 U.S.C. 1165   56

  42 U.S.C. 274   10
  42 U.S.C 406   109
  42 U.S.C 1396   110
  42 U.S.C. 1973gg-2   164
  42 U.S. C. 13951   102

STATUTES, CALIFORNIA
BUSINESS & PROFESSIONAL
  CODE ("Bus. & Prof.")
  7685   12, 16, 28
  7685.2   16, 28
  7693   28
  7695   28

STATUTES, CALIFORNIA
BUSINESS & PROFESSIONAL
  CODE ("Bus. & Prof.")
  7700   28
  7701   28
  7745   12
  9742   20

CIVIL CODE ("Civ.")
  682.1   130
  683   128-130
  1351   78, 182
  2934a   135
  2941   120, 247
  3333.2   25
  3333.4   25
  340.5   118

CIVIL PROCEDURE CODE
  ("Civ.Proc.")
  366.2   118, 176, 183
  377.60   25, 148
  685.010   176
  695.020   98
  695.030   217
  703.140   115, 158
  704.100   113
  704.115   112
  704.150   113
  704.730   114, 209
  704.995   114, 209

  1513   82
  1513.5   82
  1514   82
  1515   82
  1518   82
  1532   82

STATUTES, CALIFORNIA PROBATE CODE ("Prob.")		PROBATE CODE ("Prob.")	
52	33	3907	204
80	134, 202	3909	205
100	125, 143	3910	206
141	155	3912	206
215	111	3914	206
223	145	3915	206
224	145	3919	206
240	140, 149	3920	196
246	141	3920.5	196
250	148		
258	25	4683	2
259	148	5130	124
301	187	5134	125
331	93, 177, 218, 240, 241	5203	160
400	191	5301	202
402	191	5302	160, 201, 202, 261
403	180	5304	236, 261
1250	184, 190	5305	124
1470	219	5362	168
		5366	168
		5391	168
1500	235	5401	124
1502	235	5504	202
1513	235	5505	203
1514	235	5506	203, 261
1800.3	219	5507	160, 203
1849	29	5510	203
1849.5	29		
1850	29	6100	150
1860	219	6100.5	150
2320	219	6104	151
2610	219	6110	153
2620	219	6111	151
2640	219	6112	151, 152
3401	134	6120	92, 256
3903	205	6122	255, 256
3904	205	6122.1	255

STATUTES, CALIFORNIA PROBATE CODE ("Prob.")		REVENUE & TAXATION ("Rev. & Tax")	
13103	173	205.5	46, 211
13104	175	218	46, 211
13105	175	480	178
13109	176	5362	168
13110	176, 177	5366	168
13111	176	5391	168
13200	179, 180	13302	42
13202	180	17041	40, 81
13500	130	18566	40, 81
13550	99		
13551	99	VEHICLE CODE ("Veh.")	
13600	172	4150.5	127
13601	172	4150.7	127
13604	172	9852.5	127
13650	171	9852.7	167
13651	171	9853	73
		9853.1	73
15300	217	9853.2	73
15304	217	9853.4	73
15305	217	38012	73
15687	221	38020	73
16060	47		
16061.5	47	WELFARE AND INSTITUTIONS (Welf. & Inst.)	
17000	225	14009.5	110
20110	234		
20111	234		
21131	234		
21350	152		
21610	155, 255		
21611	155		
21620	156		

WEB SITES

CALIFORNIA WEB SITES

285 California Statutes are referenced in
Guiding Those Left Behind In California

Each state has its own set of laws relating to the settlement of a person's Estate. The laws that are referenced in this book are very different from the laws of other states.

The author is in now in the process of "translating"
Guiding Those Left Behind
for the rest of the states, that is, writing state specific books that explain how to settle the affairs of someone who dies in the given state.

Books for the following states are now in print:
ALABAMA, ARIZONA, ARKANSAS, CALIFORNIA
CONNECTICUT, FLORIDA, GEORGIA, HAWAII
ILLINOIS, INDIANA, IOWA, KANSAS
KENTUCKY, LOUISIANA, MAINE, MARYLAND
MASSACHUSETTS, MICHIGAN, MINNESOTA
MISSISSIPPI, MISSOURI, NEW JERSEY, NEW YORK
NORTH CAROLINA, OHIO, OKLAHOMA
PENNSYLVANIA, SOUTH CAROLINA, TENNESSEE
TEXAS, VIRGINIA, WASHINGTON, WISCONSIN

Call EAGLE PUBLISHING COMPANY at **(800) 824-0823** to learn of the availability of books for other states.

To order books call Eagle Publishing Company or visit our Web site for a publisher's discount.
http://www.eaglepublishing.com

BOOK REVIEWS OF *Guiding Those Left Behind*

ARIZONA

Ben T. Traywick of the Tombstone Epitaph said "This book is an excellent reference book that simplifies all the necessary tasks that must be done when there is a death in the family. There is even an explanation as to how you can arrange your own estate so that your heirs will not be left with a multitude of nagging problems." "The reviewer has been going through probate for two years with no end yet in sight. This book at the beginning two year ago would have helped immensely."

CALIFORNIA

Margot Petit Nichols of the Carmel Pine Cone called it a ". . .TRULY RIVETING READ." " . . . I could scarcely put it down." "This is a book that we should all have, either on our book shelves or thoughtfully placed with our important papers."

OTHER BOOKS BY AMELIA E. POHL

Beyond Grief To Acceptance and Peace

AMELIA E. POHL and the noted psychologist BARBARA J. SIMMONDS, Ph.d, have written a book for those families who have suffered a loss.

- ✧ What to say to the bereaved
- ✧ How to help a child through the loss
- ✧ Strategies to adjust to a new life-style
- ✧ When and where to seek assistance.

80 pages   6" X 9" $10 includes Shipping and Handling
TO ORDER CALL (800) 824-0823.

A Will Is Not Enough . . .

Many people who have a Will think that they have their affairs in order. They believe that their Will can take care of any problem that may arise. But the primary function of a Will is to distribute property to people named in a Will. A Will cannot:

⇨ Protect your assets and limit your debt

⇨ Provide care for a minor or disabled child

⇨ Avoid Guardianship

⇨ Appoint someone to make your health care decisions should you be unable to do so

⇨ Appoint someone to handle your finances should you be unable to do so

⇨ Arrange to pay for your health care should you need long term nursing care, including qualifying for MEDICAID.

AMELIA E. POHL, Esq. has written a series of state specific books explaining how to do all of these things. This new book series is a continuation of this book. It builds on basic Estate Planning concepts introduced in Chapter 7 of this book and then goes on to introduce other, more sophisticated, Estate Planning methods. Although the topics are sophisticated, the writing style is the same as in this book. It is written in plain English. It is intended for use by the average person.

A Will Is Not Enough is now available for:
ARIZONA, CALIFORNIA, COLORADO, CONNECTICUT
FLORIDA, GEORGIA, HAWAII, ILLINOIS, INDIANA, MARYLAND
MICHIGAN, MASSACHUSETTS, NEBRASKA, NEW JERSEY
NEW MEXICO, NEW YORK, OREGON, PENNSYLVANIA
TEXAS, VIRGINIA, WASHINGTON, WISCONSIN.

Visit our Web site for a Publisher's discount on any of these books.   http://www.eaglepublishing.com

How To Defend Yourself Against Your Lawyer

is a book about the unhappy experiences people have with their lawyers, beginning with that of the author AMELIA E. POHL. She became involved in a law suit and found herself in the role of client, rather than lawyer. She become concerned about lawyers who do not provide their clients with loyalty and respect. This book is a result of those concerns.

The book is divided into chapters that cover the most common problems that take people to a lawyer: divorce, probate, criminal, personal injury, starting a business, making a Will, buying a house, etc. Each chapter tells of the misadventures of the unwary as they sought the services of a lawyer without a clue as to what they were "buying." This book is funny, sad, interesting, but most of all informative. It tells the reader how to become a savvy consumer, i.e., how to find the right lawyer for the right job. If you ever find the need to employ a lawyer, you will be glad you read this book.

Copyright 2004   272 pages 6" X 9" soft cover
$20 includes Shipping and Handling

BOOK REVIEW

TED KREITER of the SATURDAY EVENING POST said "Horror fans, forget about those tawdry tales of ghosts and vampires. Pick up Amelia E. Pohl's *How To Defend Yourself Against Your Lawyer* to read some really scary stuff. Like the story . . . of the grieving widow, Ethel, whose husband died shortly after a lawyer drafted a sweetheart will for the two of them. . . . Six months in attorney's fees later, Ethel learned that she already had her husband's money because it never needed to go through probate! . . Ethel then went out and found a good lawyer for $1,000 who was able to get her $5,000 back. You do the math. . . Following Pohl's useful advice could save a person much more than money."

It is the goal of EAGLE PUBLISHING COMPANY to keep our publications fresh.

As we receive information about changes to the federal or state law we will post an update to this edition at our Web site.

http://www.eaglepublishing.com